Debating the Archaeological Heritage

Duckworth Debates in Archaeology

Series editor: Richard Hodges

Published

Debating the Archaeological Heritage
Robin Skeates

Towns and Trade in the Age of Charlemagne
Richard Hodges

Forthcoming

Loot, Legitimacy and Ownership
Colin Renfrew

Archaeology as Text
John Moreland

Celts, Germans, Scythians and Others
Peter Wells

Debating the Archaeological Heritage

Robin Skeates

Duckworth

This impression 2004
First published in 2000 by
Gerald Duckworth & Co. Ltd.
90-93 Cowcross Street, London EC1M 6BF
Tel: 020 7490 7300
Fax: 020 7490 0080
inquiries@duckworth-publishers.co.uk
www.ducknet.co.uk

A catalogue record for this book is available
from the British Library

ISBN 0 7156 2956 5

Printed and bound in Great Britain by
Antony Rowe Ltd, Eastbourne

Contents

Preface

Throughout the world, competing interest groups lay claim to the material remains of the past (Lowenthal 1990; 1995; 1998). Government officials and ethnic minorities, heritage managers and New Age religious groups, field archaeologists and looters, museum curators and indigenous peoples, critical historians and extra-terrestrialists – these are just a few examples. Groups such as these frequently clash over some fundamental questions. What is the 'archaeological heritage'? Who has the right to own, manage and interpret the material remains of the past? And how should these remains be evaluated, protected, managed, interpreted and experienced?

This book aims to provide a brief introduction to some of these contemporary debates, in six overlapping chapters that deal with defining, owning, protecting, managing, interpreting and experiencing the archaeological heritage. As such, it is intended to pull together some of the proliferating literature on 'public archaeology' and the related fields of 'cultural heritage studies' and 'museum studies'. It also offers some proposals for ethical and practical ways forward in the future, particularly for archaeologists who recurrently seem to find themselves at the centre of such debates (Gathercole & Lowenthal 1990a; Ucko 1990a). My own perspective, here, both as an archaeologist and as a lecturer in material culture and museum studies, is interdisciplinary, global and inclusive. I argue that archaeologists can no longer assume that the material remains of the past are theirs to control. Instead, they must learn more about the need for cultural sensitivity, consultation, collaboration and compromise in dealing with other interest groups (Warren 1989: 21-2). And, in particular, they must encourage the active involvement of local people with the culturally valuable material remains among which they live.

I am grateful to a number of people for helping me to complete this book. Professor Richard Hodges, the series editor, encouraged me throughout. Deborah Blake, of Duckworth, was accommodating and efficient. Valentina Vulpi, my wife, was entirely supportive and understanding. Caroline Skeates, my mother, gathered numerous press-cuttings. And Clio Hall, my daughter, indulged me with plenty of opportunities to test theory in practice. Thank you also to Sally Martin for commenting on the first chapter.

1

Defining the archaeological heritage

Before we can enter into debates surrounding the 'archaeological heritage', it is important to try to define what is meant by this and related terms such as 'archaeological resource', 'ancient monument' and 'antiquity'; particularly considering that their definitions are more vague and varied than might at first be imagined.

This is especially true of the term 'heritage', which 'all but defies definition' (Lowenthal 1998: 95). But 'heritage' (like the word 'landscape') *can* be defined in general terms, albeit on two different levels. On the one hand, 'heritage' can be used as a description of a physical entity, broadly shaped by human action (Layton & Ucko 1999: 1). On the other hand, 'heritage' can be used as an expression of the meanings, values and claims placed on that material, particularly as an 'inheritance' (Hodder 1993: 17). As part of this second definition, 'heritage' can also be regarded as a dynamic process, involving the declaration of faith in pasts that have been uncritically refashioned for present-day purposes: such as the husbanding of feelings of ancestry, continuity, identity and community; and the legitimisation of systems of power and authority (Shore 1996: 111; Lowenthal 1998). These ideas can be usefully applied to the 'archaeological heritage', which can be defined in two similar general ways. First, as the material culture of past societies that survives in the present; and second, as the process through

9

which the material culture of past societies is re-evaluated and re-used in the present. At the final analysis, it is pointless to argue over which of these two definitions is correct, since both are established usages (Layton & Ucko 1999: 2).

However, it is interesting to note who uses which definition. Critical historians are now promoting the second, conceptual, definition of the 'archaeological heritage'. By contrast, national governments, cultural agencies and professional bodies still cling to the first, descriptive, definition of the 'archaeological heritage'; despite (or perhaps because of) the fact that they actively dominate the re-evaluation and re-use of it in the present. These organisations authoritatively claim the right to declare the 'archaeological heritage' as such: defining what material is culturally significant and what is not; what material is to be studied, listed and preserved and what is to be left to decay or destroyed (Ucko 1990a: xv). But at the same time their employees are faced with serious practical difficulties in making those selections and designations, even when the 'archaeological heritage' is defined simply as a physical entity (e.g. Lipe 1984: 1-2; García Sanjuán & Wheatley 1999: 211-13). For example, the scale of any element of the 'archaeological heritage' (in terms of the number, variety and spatial extent of examples of it) is always difficult to define. Also, individuals can evaluate these elements differently according to their different perspectives and interests. These practical problems faced by professionals are exacerbated by competing interest groups who sometimes call 'official' definitions into question, as part of attempts to have their own 'cultural heritage' officially recognised as such. A certain degree of subjectivity and even bias is, then, inherent in the definition of the 'archaeological heritage'.

This becomes clear when one examines, in more detail, examples of different definitions of the 'archaeological heritage', and related terms, promoted by different interest-groups throughout the world. Here, I shall consider statements published by: an international agency, a national government and agency, a body of professional archaeologists and a group of indigenous people.

Alternative definitions

The United Nations Educational, Scientific and Cultural Organisation (UNESCO), in their *Convention Concerning the Protection of the World Cultural and Natural Heritage*, first published in 1972, broadly defines 'heritage' as an inheritance, 'our legacy from the past, what we live with today, and what we pass on to future generations' (UNESCO 1997). However, they use the term 'cultural heritage' in a more restricted way, to refer to: 'monuments, groups of buildings and sites with historical, aesthetic, archaeological, scientific, ethnological or anthropological value' (ibid.). Their definition of the term 'World Heritage Site' is then narrower still, with its emphasis on 'the best possible examples' of the cultural heritage, of 'outstanding universal value' (ibid.). In more detail, they state that the cultural properties of a 'World Heritage Site', worthy of inclusion in the 'World Heritage List', should:

(i) 'represent a masterpiece of human creative genius', or

(ii) 'exhibit an important interchange of human values over a span of time or within a cultural area of the world, on developments in architecture or technology, monumental arts, town planning or landscape design', or

(iii) 'bear a unique or at least exceptional testimony to a cultural tradition or to a civilisation which is living or has disappeared', or

(iv) 'be an outstanding example of a type of building or architectural or technological ensemble, or landscape which illustrates a significant stage or significant stages in human history', or

(v) 'be an outstanding example of a traditional human settlement or land-use which is representative of a culture or cultures, especially when it has become vulnerable under the impact of irreversible change', or

(vi) 'be directly or tangibly associated with events or living traditions, with ideas or with beliefs, or with artistic and literary works of outstanding universal significance' (a criterion used only in exceptional circumstances, and together with other criteria).

Also, 'Equally important is the authenticity of the site and the way it is protected and managed'. (ibid.)

Although seemingly written in stone, these definitions must be considered critically. Seen in a positive light, they reflect UNESCO's worthy global perspective towards humanity. But from a more negative point of view, they also strongly reflect and fossilise the political ideals and academic interests of UNESCO's advisors in the late 1960s and early 70s. Furthermore, in practice, 'the development of the World Heritage List since the first inscriptions in 1978 has been piecemeal' (Cleere 1995: 67). It has tended to over-represent the industrialised world, historical cities and periods, Christian religious monuments and 'elitist' architecture, at the expense of traditional living cultures and non-monumental structures, which also comprise part of the world's cultural heritage.

National governments, through their laws and cultural agencies, define the 'archaeological heritage' differently, with an emphasis on individual 'antiquities', 'sites', 'monuments' and 'resources' of national significance, that are generally older than 100 years (Cleere 1984). In England, for example, the *Ancient Monuments and Archaeological Areas Act* of 1979 and 1983 defines a 'monument' as:

1. Defining the archaeological heritage

(a) 'any building, structure or work, whether above or below the surface of the land, and any cave or excavation';

(b) 'any site comprising the remains of any such building, structure or work or of any cave or excavation'; and

(c) 'any site comprising, or comprising the remains of, any vehicle, vessel, aircraft or other movable structure or part thereof which neither constitutes nor forms art of any work which is a monument within paragraph (a) above';

and 'any machinery attached to a monument ... if it could not be detached without being dismantled.' (Her Majesty's Government 1983: 63).

In accordance with this law, scheduling of monuments of 'national importance' is carried out by English Heritage, who employ the following standard selection criteria:

(a) 'Period – How representative is this type of monument of its period in history or prehistory, and how long was it in use?';

(b) 'Rarity and representativity – How rare is this type of monument, both regionally and nationally? Does it have an importance as a good example of the commonplace and most typical?'

(c) 'Diversity of form – Are there variations in the type of monument specific to its region or period?'

(d) 'Survival – How well does the monument survive, both above and below ground?'

(e) 'Group value – Is the monument associated with other sites of the same period, or is it part of a sequence of sites which has developed through time?'

(f) 'Potential – What potential has the site to teach us about the past? Can we predict if it is likely to contain as yet undiscovered archaeological evidence?'

(g) 'Documentation – Are there any historical records of the monument, or any modern surveys or studies such as excavation reports?'

(h) 'Diversity of feature – How many features characteristic of its class does the monument include: i.e. how complete is it, is there also evidence for successive types of use?'

Additional factors include: 'if a particular monument ... is already accessible to the public; the vulnerability and fragility of the monument; the practicality of maintaining it; and if scheduling would in fact help to achieve long-term preservation' (English Heritage 1997).

Again, these definitions and selection criteria must be considered critically. The evident precision and openness with which archaeological sites of national significance are defined and selected for scheduling in England is surely to be commended. However, the representativeness of the resultant list of 'scheduled ancient monuments' has been questioned (e.g. Carver 1996; Fairclough 1996). For example, according to the *Ancient Monuments and Archaeological Areas Act*, urban areas cannot usually be scheduled (with the exception of castles, monastic sites and urban defences); neither can buildings in ecclesiastical use, such as historic churches and cathedrals; and neither can some early prehistoric sites that are visible only as surface or ploughsoil scatters of stone artefacts. As a consequence, 'English heritage' tends to be presented to the public, and to tourists in particular, as a narrow range of relatively spectacular structural remains, which commonly include prehistoric tombs, stone circles and hillforts; Roman villas and military installations; and medieval abbeys, castles and palaces (Champion 1996: 140). This is becoming increasingly problematic, not only in archaeological terms, but also in the context of contemporary multicultural 'English' society (Hodder 1990).

Bodies of professional archaeologists, through their principles and codes of ethics and conduct, also define the 'archaeological heritage' in their own specific terms. For example, the Institute of Field Archaeologists' *Code of Conduct* of 1993 defines the 'archaeological heritage' as 'the material remains of man's activities' and as 'a finite, vulnerable and diminishing resource' (Institute of Field Archaeologists 1995: 14). The Ethics in Archaeology Committee of the Society of American Archaeology, in their *Principles of Archaeological Ethics* of 1995, also defines the 'archaeological record' as: '*in situ* archaeological material and sites, archaeological collections, records, and reports' (Vitelli 1996b: 264). Despite their apparent neutrality, these particular definitions clearly form part of a strategy to encourage and maintain high standards of professional archaeological practice.

Groups of indigenous peoples around the world are increasingly questioning the validity of such Western definitions of the 'archaeological heritage'. This is occurring particularly in cases where these groups' traditional landscapes and cultural activities within them, some of which have been materially ephemeral, are either included or excluded officially as elements of national heritage. Australian Aborigines, for example, have criticised state laws for the protection of Aboriginal sites, with reference to 'their underlying premise that the recording of traditional sites should be based on their treatment as relics of the past and not as places with living cultural value' (Ritchie 1994: 227). In Victoria, for instance, the *Archaeological and Aboriginal Relics Preservation Act* of 1972 defines a 'relic' as: 'any Aboriginal deposit, carving, drawing, skeletal remains and anything belonging to the total body of material relating to that past Aboriginal occupation of Australia' (ibid.: 229). Attempts by the Heritage Commission to construct a *Register of the National Estate*, including only 'sites which were the most outstanding Aboriginal places deserving of national recognition', also met with resistance from Aboriginal people, who 'were often loath to enter into an argument which started from the assumption that gradings of value should be made within the overall concept of the sanctity of the entire earth' (Ucko 1994: xix).

Cultural heritage

These examples indicate that different, and sometimes competing, interest groups actively maintain a variety of concepts, ideals, interests, priorities and strategies in relation to the definition of the 'archaeological heritage'. In doing so, they all (often unwittingly) participate within the 'heritage process', through which the material culture of past societies is re-evaluated and re-used in the present.

In general, all of these groups have tended not to be self-critical: choosing, instead, to present their definitions of the 'archaeological heritage' as authoritative statements of law or policy. But recently, changes in policy (but not law), have begun to appear in response to some of the criticisms raised above. UNESCO, to its credit, has begun to recognise and rectify some of the problems relating to its World Heritage List. It has begun to incorporate 'extrinsic' cultural and socio-economic values into its management guidelines for World Heritage Sites (Feilden & Jokilehto 1993). It has also held regional meetings in under-represented parts of the world (such as Ethiopia and Fiji) and thematic meetings on under-represented subjects (such as heritage canals and Asian rice culture), in order to identify and nominate new World Heritage Sites. For example, in 1992 the World Heritage Committee recognised the 'outstanding universal value' of cultural landscapes, which had previously fallen between the categories of 'cultural' and 'natural' heritage. This, then, allowed the inclusion of the landscapes of non-urban and non-monumental cultures, and the consequent enhancement of their protection and management (Cleere 1995). In England, too, organisations such as English Heritage have begun to face up to the problem of their unrepresentative records of 'monuments'. For example, there has been a dramatic increase in the recording of previously neglected post-medieval remains in England over the last decade. This reflects both an increasing use of early maps and documentary research to supplement traditional field-based archaeological sources of information, and an expanding professional definition of what constitutes the 'archaeological heritage' (Darvill & Fulton 1998: 4). Some changes have also occurred in Australia as a result of Aboriginal peoples' protests. For example, in 1990 the National Aboriginal Sites Authorities Committee, the national body representing the various government authorities charged with the protection of Aboriginal sites, finally acknowledged that there had previously been an undue emphasis on what they termed 'archaeological sites', as opposed to those sites which continued to be of significance to living Aboriginal people (Ritchie 1994: 233, 237).

Two new ways forward can, now, be proposed in relation to debates surrounding the definition of the 'archaeological heritage'. The first concerns selection policies, particularly on a national scale (Cleere 1984: 126-7; Deebden et al. 1999: 182). Given that it is simply a Utopian dream to consider that all past material culture can be preserved for ever, we must devise clear policies for the selection of a representative sample of material to be recorded, preserved and protected for the future, based on reliable estimations of the nature and extent of the total archaeological database. The second way forward concerns the abandonment of the term 'archaeological' when applied to 'heritage', particularly on a global scale. As Susan Sullivan, the Executive Director of the Australian Heritage Commission, has pointed out: the value of past material (including 'sites' and 'monuments') is not just 'archaeological' (Stanley Price & Sullivan 1995: 130-1). This is the definition ascribed to that material by archaeologists, who assume it to be their right to define, study and control it. But for other interest groups, including

17

indigenous people and tourists, these remains are primarily cultural and symbolic, and as such they are better defined simply as malleable elements of 'cultural heritage'.

2

Owning the archaeological heritage

Claims of property and of ownership placed upon the material remains of past societies comprise a particularly controversial aspect of the heritage process, in which those remains are re-evaluated and re-used in the present. This is because they raise some fundamental questions. For example: Can the material remains of the past be 'owned' as 'property', either public or private? (Warren 1989: 14-15; Prott & O'Keefe 1992). If so, who has the right to designate and to claim them as such (Ucko 1990a: xvi)? And if they are deemed to be held in the wrong hands, should they be given back to their rightful guardians?

Different answers to these questions are provided by often competing interest groups. These include: national governments; the United Nations Educational, Scientific and Cultural Organisation (UNESCO); professional archaeologists and physical anthropologists; museum curators; private collectors; and indigenous peoples.

National governments often claim ownership of all or certain categories of past material culture found or rightfully held within their territories, particularly as part of legal regimes intended to protect the national patrimony. For example, the 1964 *Antiquities Law* of Cyprus states that, 'Subject to the provisions of this Law, all antiquities lying undiscovered at the date of the coming into operation of this Law in or upon any land shall be the property of the Government' (O'Keefe 1997: 34). A similar law exists in Italy (Law No. 1089 of 1939), although, here, privately owned ruins surviving above ground and objects found prior to 1939 are exempt (D'Agostino 1984: 76). This concept of state-owned cultural property has been accepted uncritically by UNESCO (Merriman 1986). However, following its 1954 (Hague) *Convention for the Protection of Cultural Property in the Event of Armed Conflict*, UNESCO has claimed that key elements of national cultural property can also form part of 'the cultural heritage of all mankind' (Lowenthal 1998: 228). In 1960, for example, the Director-General of UNESCO, Vittorini Veronese, launching an international appeal for funds to help save the ancient Egyptian monuments of Abu Simbel, claimed that, these 'wonderous structures, ranking among the most magnificent on earth ... do not belong solely to the countries which hold them in trust. The whole world has a right to see them endure. They are part of a common heritage ... entitled to universal protection' (Chamberlin 1979: 178). This perspective was enshrined soon after in UNESCO's 1972 *Convention Concerning the Protection of the World Cultural and Natural Heritage*, which claims that sites which have been inscribed on the World Heritage List constitute, 'without prejudice to national sovereignty or ownership', 'World Heritage Sites' that 'belong to all the peoples of the world, irrespective of the territory on which they are located' (UNESCO 1997).

Professional archaeologists and physical anthropologists generally accept these overlapping concepts of national and universal ownership, at the same time as recognising that they rarely own the material culture of past societies that they discover and investigate (e.g. Vitelli 1996b: 264). However, they have frequently assumed that those 'archaeological data' are their property on an intellectual basis, and that they and museum curators are their primary guardians (e.g. Lynott & Wylie 1995: 23).

Such assumptions have been questioned increasingly by indigenous 'first' peoples, who often 'see care of the past as a duty and responsibility', and who also have 'firm ideas as to what behaviour is appropriate' with regard to their ancestral remains (Tsosie 1997: 66). For a start, they have traditionally approached the concepts of property ownership and heritage from a different perspective. The Suquamish American Indians, for example, 'see archaeological sites as belonging to past, present and future generations; there is no way to own the site or the material within them' (Forsman 1997: 107). They have also traditionally expressed their rights to cultural resources, including both restricted sacred sites and objects and extensive territories, not with reference to legal documents, but though cultural connection, descendancy and occupancy (Gathercole & Lowenthal 1990b: 91-2). Furthermore, indigenous peoples, ethnic minorities and newly independent nations, who have frequently been dispossessed of their land, religion and language by European colonial settlers and governments, often cherish their ancestral relics as icons of group identity and freedom, particularly within an international political context of indigenous rights movements and post-colonialism, and they have therefore demanded the restitution of their cultural property with increasing vociferousness (Lowenthal 1990: 308-9).

These general opinions and debates have been rehearsed in a diversity of situations throughout the world, and have consequently taken on many different dimensions. In an attempt to express something of this complexity, I shall now consider two key examples of the restitution debate. These concern: the treatment of the bones and material culture of indigenous peoples and minority groups in the USA; and the curation of the 'Parthenon Marbles' in the British Museum.

Cultural remains of indigenous peoples and minority groups in the USA

In the USA, the ownership, curation, restitution and reburial of Native American human remains has, over the last 25 years, been the principal and most contentious matter discussed between archaeologists and American Indians (Downer 1997: 24, 30). The subjects of this debate are the estimated half a million Indian bodies that have been, or still are, stored and displayed in museums, universities and archaeological laboratories in the United States, and the additional half a million Indian bodies curated in similar contexts in European countries (Hammil & Cruz 1989: 195). Many of these were obtained through archaeological excavations of Indian cemetery areas. Such activities were legally condoned by the Antiquities Act of 1906, which was intended to protect archaeological sites on federal and tribal lands from looters. It defined the remains of dead Indians, buried on federal lands, as 'archaeological resources', 'objects of historic and scientific interest', and as 'federal property'. Thus, under federal law, it was entirely possible to disinter Indian bodies and to deposit them in permanent museum collections (Tsosie 1997: 68).

Since the mid-1960s, American Indians and their supporters have become increasingly concerned over such excavations and the public display of Indian bones in museums and related institutions, and they have actively sought the restitution and reburial of these bones (e.g. Anderson 1985; Hubert 1989; Zimmerman 1989a). One of the fundamental issues here is that American Indians perceive such bones to be the sacred remains of their ancestors, who are regarded as living spiritual entities, occupying ancestral sites (White Deer 1997). One of them would say, then, that, 'I see people, I do not see bones' (Hubert 1989: 132). The removal of these bones and associated grave goods from the ground, and the disturbance of their sacred burial sites, American Indians argue, offends against their basic human rights to religious freedom and spiritual fulfilment, in yet another example of their cultural exploitation and repression by members of the dominant Euro-American, Christian, population (e.g. McIntosh et al. 1989; Tsosie 1997). Furthermore, by the collection and display of this skeletal material, 'Native Americans were made to feel like specimens' (Lippert 1997: 121).

These points were highlighted in a test-case in the early 1970s in Iowa, where an Indian skeleton was found on the edge of a white pioneer cemetery which lay on the route of a planned highway (Anderson 1985; Zimmerman 1989a). In line with standard archaeological procedures, the State Archaeologist, Marshall McKusick, removed the Indian bones to a laboratory at the University of Iowa for study, but authorised the immediate exhumation and reburial of the white peoples' bones. An Indian activist, Running Moccasins (Maria Pearson), publicised and contested this differential treatment of the bones, gaining support from other Indians, churches and students, and eventually succeeded in obtaining a court order for the reburial of the Indian bones.

Since then, Native American support for the reburial movement has grown. This is reflected, for example, by the organisation known as American Indians Against Desecration (AIAD), which is 'a project of the International Indian Treaty Council ... with delegates representing some 97 Indian tribes and Nations from across North and South America' (Hammil & Cruz 1989: 195). However, it would be misleading to suggest that there is one Native American interpretation concerning the appropriate treatment of human remains and ancestral sites. 'There are as many interpretations as there are tribal governments, religious groups within tribes, and political movements among tribes' (Tsosie 1997: 64). For this reason, it is often more accurate to discuss specific tribes rather than the generic

'Native Americans' (Ferguson et al. 1997: 238). Matters have been further complicated by the fact that many of the people coming forward to demand repatriation have been members of the new radical Indian movement, rather than traditional Indian spokespeople, such as tribal elders, medicine people and spiritual leaders (Downer 1997: 31).

American archaeologists and physical anthropologists, for their part, have, in general, self-confidently assumed their scientific perspective to be authoritative and unchallengeable (Zimmerman 1989b: 215). They have regarded human remains to be an important, and often unique, source of scientific data about such things as patterns of disease in past populations, diet, adaptation to the environment, biological changes, mortuary practices and social relations (Hubert 1989: 131). More generally, they have equated the Indian with the past: viewing all Indian remains as ancient; and assuming all Indian archaeological sites to have been abandoned by their former occupants (McGuire 1989: 180-1). They have also pointed out, with some pride, that their research on Indian bones has been of benefit to contemporary Native Americans: contributing to a greater understanding of their prehistoric past; helping to dispel racist myths about the capacities of Native Americans by demonstrating that their ancestors built the mound sites of the mid-continent and the cliff-dwellings of the south-west; and providing crucial evidence in tribal land claims (e.g. Meighan 1994). They have therefore argued that scientific access to permanent museum collections of skeletal material exerts prior claim over the cultural beliefs and religious freedom of living populations, and that, with reburial, a vital source of information about the past would no longer be available for study (McIntosh et al. 1989: 79). Such views continue to be expressed by hard-core archaeological activists, including members of the American Committee for Preservation of Archaeological Collections (ACPAC).

2. Owning the archaeological heritage

During the late-1970s and 1980s, some attempts were made to resolve these conflicts between American Indians and archaeologists, although they remained dominated by archaeological interests. Many States established consultative bodies with local Indian communities to discuss ways in which archaeological research could continue, with reburial as the eventual outcome; and several also introduced new legislation (Hubert 1989: 141). The State of Iowa again led the way (Anderson 1985). In 1976, the *Iowa Code* was changed, with the endorsement of local archaeologists. Basically, this statute did four things: (1) strengthened the legal protection of ancient cemetery areas; (2) clarified the primary responsibility of the State Archaeologist in co-ordinating investigations; (3) provided a contingency fund to pay for the recovery of human skeletal remains; and (4) established a state cemetery for the re-interment of 'ancient' (i.e. more than 150 years old) human skeletal remains. From the Native American perspective this was not ideal, since they did not want their ancestors' graves disturbed at all, but they did accept that newly uncovered human remains would have to be studied in order to determine their racial or cultural affiliation prior to reburial. This basic mutual understanding was enhanced by a series of conferences, seminars and meetings. As a consequence, by 1985, Indians in Iowa were involved with professional archaeologists and anthropologists in a variety of co-operative projects: serving as advisers to the Iowa Department of Transportation on matters concerning the accidental unearthing of ancient cemeteries; negotiating with government resource agencies for rulings favourable to the protection and presentation of ancient sites; taking part in archaeological fieldwork; participating in the presentation of public programs sponsored by state and federal humanities agencies; and obtaining help from anthropologists in preserving their tribal treasures. The federal *Archaeological Resources Protection Act* (ARPA) of 1979 only partially reflected this shift in attitude towards Native American bones: by designating Native American human remains and cultural items as tribal property, in cases where they had been excavated on tribal lands; although it still defined them as 'archaeological resources' and as 'federal property', of historic and scientific interest to the general public, in cases where they were excavated on federal lands (Tsosie 1997: 69). Ultimately, this Act remained heavily biased towards the interests of archaeologists. For their part, only a few archaeologists took a more self-critical perspective. Larry Zimmerman, for example, recognised his obligations to the people whose pasts he studied, and 'came to accept reburial as scientifically, professionally, and personally ethical' (Zimmerman 1989a: 60). So too did the Society of Professional Archaeologists (SOPA), who included in their 1981 *Code of Ethics* a statement that archaeologists should be, 'sensitive to, and respect the legitimate concerns of, groups whose culture histories are the subjects of archaeological investigations' (Zimmerman 1997: 51).

To many archaeologists these developments seemed sufficient, but by the late-1980s Native American rights activists had gathered sufficient momentum to take their fundamental charge of inequality in religious human rights, and in the treatment of Caucasian and Native American human remains, all the way to the top. Their appeal led to the signing of the *Native American Graves Protection and Repatriation Act* (NAGPRA) by President Bush in 1990. NAGPRA has six basic provisions: (1) it requires federal agencies and private museums which receive federal funds to inventory their collections of Native American human remains and associated grave goods; (2) it states that tribes have ownership of all human remains and cultural items found on tribal or federal land; (3) it prohibits trafficking in human remains and cultural items; (4) it requires museums to create summaries of unassociated funerary objects, sacred objects and objects of cultural patrimony; (5)

it requires these inventories and summaries to be sent to all federally recognised tribes according to a specified timetable; and (6) it authorises these tribes to reclaim identifiable human remains and objects of ceremonial significance when they can prove 'cultural affiliation' or can show that the museum obtained the remains without the legal consent of the owner (Pinkerton 1992). As a result, some such repatriations have taken place, but not on the large scale first predicted by museum curators and archaeologists (Downer 1997: 32). For example, in 1999, in accordance with NAGPRA, the bones of nearly 2000 people and over 500 funerary objects were returned by Harvard University and the Phillips Andover Academy to the residents of the pueblo of Jemez in New Mexico, who consequently reburied the bones in a mass grave in the national park (Slayman 1999b: 17).

NAGPRA represents a compromise between Native Americans, museum curators and archaeologists, and its precise meanings and implications are still being debated by all of them, particularly as part of the process of attempting to put it into practice (Tsosie 1997: 70-1). Some archaeologists remain angry or at least suspicious about NAGPRA (Zimmerman 1997: 48). They have criticised it, claiming that it will impair their ability to research past cultures, and that repatriation of remains to contemporary Indians is unjustified because the connections between ancient and modern Indian cultures are too tenuous. Native Americans, for their part, have generally celebrated NAGPRA's acknowledgement of their legal rights and cultural claims, and its attempt to redress past wrongs perpetrated by scientists in the acquisition of skeletal remains and grave goods (Merriman & Rightmire 1995: 18). However, they too have expressed criticisms, and many remain wary of archaeologists. From their perspective, tribes are limited as to what they can repossess under NAGPRA, because it applies only to excavations on federal or tribal lands (as opposed to state or private property), and to objects held in federal or federally-funded institutions (as opposed to private collections). Furthermore, NAGPRA still authorises the intentional archaeological excavation of human remains, funerary objects, sacred objects and objects of cultural patrimony, if these objects are removed in accordance with all permit requirements, and so long as notification and consultation with the affected Indian tribes occurs prior to excavation. And even objects required to be repatriated to tribes may still be studied and subjected to scientific testing before their return. Thus, from an indigenous perspective, NAGPRA provides only limited protection for Native American interests in preventing the desecration of ancestral sites and remains. Another practical problem, shared by all parties, is in demonstrating a relationship between the claimants and the materials claimed. This is far from simple in states such as Oklahoma, where members of the large Indian population belong to 37 different federally recognised tribes, which include indigenous and removed groups, with distinct historical origins, political systems, cultural values and traditional practices (Brooks 1997: 209-10). Such differences, as well as disputes over resources, have directly contributed to a lack of accord among south-western tribes over the cultural affinity of historical populations to present-day tribes (Swidler & Cohen 1997: 205).

Some of these post-NAGPRA tensions are clearly reflected in the case of 'Kennewick Man' (Whittell 1997; Hiscock 1998; Lee 1999a; 1999b; 1999c). In 1996, the well-preserved remains of an ancient skeleton, with a stone projectile point embedded in its pelvis, were discovered in Columbia Park, on the banks of the Columbia River, in Kennewick, Washington State. They were radiocarbon dated to around 9200 years old. A legal battle developed between physical anthropologists and four Indian tribes, including the local Umatilla. The anthropologists have claimed that further study of the bones could transform their knowledge of how North America was originally populated, and some of them have even claimed that they belong to a 'Caucasoid' human with European features and even white skin. The American Indians, on the other hand, have claimed that the remains are indigenous, and have demanded that 'the Ancient One' be re-buried in accordance with Indian religion and NAGPRA federal law. The site of the discovery was consequently covered over by the US Army's Corps of Engineers to prevent erosion and looting, despite objections from both the scientists and the Indian tribes; and the remains were seized by federal authorities. Detailed scientific analyses of the bones, including additional radiocarbon dating, were then commissioned from an independent group of federal agencies, in an attempt to clarify who the bones belong to. Initial reports, based on studies carried out at the Burke Museum in Seattle, suggest that Kennewick Man is physically closer to south-east Asian populations than to modern Indians or Caucasians.

Following the example of the American Indians, African Americans in the USA have also become increasingly concerned with the archaeological treatment of the bones of their ancestors, as part of a broader struggle for empowerment. An important example is the controversy which surrounded the archaeological excavation of the Colonial African Burial Ground in New York City in the early-1990s (Harrington 1993). This eighteenth-century cemetery contained the remains of an estimated 10,000 to 20,000 people, both black and lower-class white. A section of it lay under a parking lot, just two blocks north of New York's City Hall, which was acquired in 1990 by the General Services Administration (GSA), a federal agency which planned to build a government office tower and pavilion on the area. As part of the re-development process, GSA hired Historic Conservation and Interpretation (HCI), an archaeological consultancy and salvage firm, to excavate some 420 skeletons from the site between 1991 and 1992. HCI transferred these bones to Lehman College in the Bronx, where they underwent conservation. These actions attracted angry protests from the city's black community, which felt that its concerns were not being addressed by white bureaucrats in their decisions about the excavation and disposition of its heritage. The black activists made various conflicting demands: some wanted the exhumation to stop, others wanted a museum built on the site, and others wanted nothing there. Eventually, the congressional House Subcommittee on Public Buildings and Grounds, acting on the advice of New York City's first black mayor, halted the excavation of the burial ground. Then, following further lobbying of Congress from the city's black community, President Bush signed *Public Law 102-393*, ordering the GSA to cease construction of the pavilion portion of the project, and approving a $3 million grant for the construction of a museum honouring the contribution of African Americans to colonial New York City. The GSA also set up a federal advisory committee, chaired by Howard Dodson of New York's Schomburg Centre for Research in Black Culture, to address plans for the reburial of the human remains, an African Burial Ground Memorial, and a burial-ground exhibition in the central office tower.

The Parthenon Marbles

The British Museum and its rights of ownership and control over some of the most important archaeological treasures in its collection are the subject of other long-running restitution debates. The classic example here is the Parthenon or 'Elgin' Marbles. This collection of marble sculptures from the Parthenon in Athens, thought to have been carved under the eye if not also the hand of the famous classical Greek sculptor Phidias, was bought from Lord Elgin by the British Government for the British Museum in 1816. It has been the subject of restitution claims ever since. The following background paragraphs are based on William St.Clair's recent and authoritative book on the history of the collection (St.Clair 1998).

Lord Elgin obtained the marbles whilst serving as the British Ambassador to the Sultan of Turkey in Constantinople. His original plan had been to send professional artists, architects and moulders to Athens to obtain drawings, measurements and plaster casts of the classical Greek monuments surviving on the Acropolis, in order to improve the knowledge of Greek architecture in Great Britain. Elgin successfully obtained official letters (firmans) for this work from the Ottoman government in 1801, at a time when the British were favoured by the Turks, following their joint defeat of Bonaparte's French force in Egypt. Two firmans were consequently dispatched to Athens, which overruled the decisions of local officials, including the Voivode (governor) and Distar (military governor of the Acropolis), who had previously refused to allow Elgin's artists on to the Acropolis. The second firman, drawn up by Philip Hunt, Elgin's chaplain and private secretary, included permission to remove obstructions from the monuments, and to conduct excavations, taking away anything of interest which the excavations yielded, but there was no mention of taking anything from the buildings themselves. Hunt acted as courier for this document, delivering it to the Voivode who consequently assured him that Lord Elgin's agents would have all the facilities which the firman conferred. Hunt then immediately pressed home his advantage, and, with the aid of gifts, persuaded the Voivode to grant him permission to take down one of the metopes from the Parthenon. Hunt later confirmed that both he and the Voivode had realised that the terms of the second firman were being exceeded, but that questions of legality or of propriety scarcely arose. Once this initial permission for removals had been granted, all the authorities in Athens co-operated fully with Elgin's agents, who oversaw the removal of numerous sculptures (including metopes, slabs of the frieze and figures from the pediments) and architectural fragments from the Parthenon, and their export by boat from Piraeus to England. Elgin encouraged this work of removal, both from Constantinople and during a personal visit to Athens in 1802, and on his return to Constantinople he obtained official letters from the Ottoman government, legitimating any illegalities perpetrated under the terms of the second firman.

Elgin eventually returned to Britain in 1806. He was deeply in debt, particularly as a result of expenditure on his collection, and in 1810 he finally decided that he would have to try to sell it to the British Government. In response, the Government decided that it was prepared to recommend to Parliament that the collection be bought for £30,000, but Elgin rejected this offer as too low. Then, in 1812, Lord Byron, the philhellenic idealist, published *Childe Harold's Pilgrimage*. In it, Byron asserted an ancestral connection between the modern Greeks of the nineteenth century and ancient Greeks of the classical age, and questioned Elgin's right to damage and remove the precious, two thousand-year-old heritage of the proud but enslaved nation of Greece. This text became one of the most popular poems of the nineteenth century, and it helped not only to establish the Parthenon as a icon of national identity, but also to blacken the name of Lord Elgin. Elgin, for his part, was more concerned with starting a new campaign to sell his collection, and in 1814 he re-approached the Government. At his instigation, the Government set up a Select Committee of the House of Commons to investigate the circumstances in which the collection had been obtained and to advise on whether, and at what price, the nation should acquire them. The Report of the Committee vindicated Elgin from the main charges of illegality, misuse of ambassadorial powers, unnecessary damage to the monuments, and desire to make money and recommended a price of £35,000 for the marbles. Lord Elgin had little alternative but to accept, and in 1816 Parliament voted in favour of the sale and sum by the narrowest of margins. An Act of Parliament was then duly passed which transferred the ownership of the Elgin Marbles to the nation and their custody to the British Museum in London.

In addition to repeated demands from the Greek Government for the return of the marbles, a number of arguments have been proposed in support of their restitution to Athens (Hitchins 1987; St.Clair 1998). (1) Their local contextual significance. The sculptures were set up on the outside of a local Athenian temple to commemorate the local myths and traditions of the city and to proclaim the power and distinctiveness of its culture. Removed from their original setting, they therefore lose meaning and value. (2) The illegality of the removal of the Marbles. The second firman of 1801 conferred no authority to remove sculptures from the Parthenon buildings or to damage them, and both Hunt and the Voivode realised this. It is also probable that neither the Voivode nor the Distar had the legal authority to exceed the powers given by the second firman, or to give permission for the removals on their own authority. Indeed, the Turks later declared, in 1809, that Elgin had never had permission to remove any marbles, and that the activities of his agents at Athens had been illegal from the start. The Greek government also argued, after the establishment of the Greek state in 1833, that the marbles were Greek property, stolen by a foreign ambassador to an alien occupying power. (3) The lack of care with which the Marbles have been treated in the British Museum, at least on one occasion. In 1938, on the orders of Sir Joseph Duveen, the museum's millionaire benefactor, the marbles were scraped 'clean' using copper tools and a piece of coarse carborundum, which resulted in the irrecoverable loss of a large proportion of their original surfaces. Despite newspaper rumours about this damage, the Trustees of the Museum publicly claimed that nothing much had happened, and in the re-display of the Marbles the public was prevented from taking too close a look. (4) The misleading display of the Marbles in the British Museum. The display in the Duveen Gallery gives a misleading idea of the size, shape and colour of the Parthenon and its sculptures, by its re-arrangement of the sculptures in a false symmetry and with their outsides facing in, and by the use of coloured spotlights which exaggerate the shadows. (5) The importance of the Acropolis in Athens, including its architecture and sculptures, as the supreme modern Greek symbol of national identity and continuity. In March 1935, the Acropolis was declared a national monument, located in the heart of the new capital of the new Kingdom of Greece. Since then, according to Melina Mercouri, the Greek Minister of Culture and restitution campaigner, the people of Greece have come to regard the Parthenon as the 'soul of Greece'. (6) Neil Kinnock's promise, when Leader of the Opposition, to return the Marbles. He claimed that, 'the Parthenon without the Marbles is like a smile with a missing tooth' (Reynolds 1996). (7) The Greek authorities' ability to look after the Marbles. Drawing upon Greek and European Union resources, the Greek authorities have now begun work (in 1995) on a purpose-built New Acropolis Museum, which will be able to curate the Marbles, and within sight of the Acropolis. (8) British public opinion favours the return of the Marbles. According to a Channel 4 television poll carried out in 1996, 93% of viewers supported proposals for the return of the Marbles. Also, according to a MORI poll, carried out in 1998, around 66% of the public and around 52% of Members of Parliament would vote in favour of sending the Marbles back to Greece.

A series of counter-arguments have also been made as to why the Marbles should remain in the British Museum (e.g. Wilson 1989: 114-16). (1) Permissions were granted for the removal of the Marbles and for their appropriation by Lord Elgin. The Voivode of Athens initially granted permission to Hunt to remove them from the buildings on the Acropolis, and the Turkish and Greek authorities co-operated with this decision. Lord Elgin then obtained letters from the Ottoman government which confirmed those decisions taken by the Voivode and Distar. And, in 1810, authority was granted by the Kaymacam to allow those sculptures from the Parthenon that still remained in Ottoman territory to be sent to Elgin in Britain. All of this was confirmed by the British Government's *Select Committee's Report* of 1816, which vindicated Elgin from the charge of illegality. Modern experts in international law have also usually agreed that, 'Elgin's actions were probably technically lawful in the circumstances of the time, that his claim to personal ownership and right to sell were valid in law, and that any action by Greece, as successor government, to try to recover the marbles in an international court would probably fail' (St.Clair 1998: 157). (2) Modern Greeks' claims of cultural continuity with the ancient Greeks are false. As in many other European states, Greece's tradition of national and cultural continuity was invented in the nineteenth century. (3) The removal of the Marbles from the Parthenon and their curation in the British Museum has helped to save them from various threats in Athens. Prior to Elgin's interventions, the Parthenon had already been damaged during its use as a Turkish military installation, and Western European souvenir-hunters had already begun to remove sculptured fragments from the Parthenon. And from the 1960s, serious air pollution in the Athens basin had 'done more damage to the essential constituents of the Parthenon than any single previous catastrophe' (ibid: 329). (4) In accordance with the British Government's *Museums Act* of 1963, the British Museum is, by law, forbidden to part with any of its property. (5) The British Museum regards itself as a 'universal museum', which holds cultural material in trust for the whole of mankind. (6) If the Marbles were returned, the floodgates of restitution might be opened. All of the major museums of the world might come under pressure to disperse their important international collections.

The current situation is that the debate continues (Born 1999; Brysac 1999; Nightingale 1999; Smith 1999; Woolf 1999). Despite Neil Kinnock's promise to return the Marbles, the incoming Labour government, in 1997, rejected a renewed restitution request from the Greek government. The British Minister of Culture, Chris Smith, claimed that the Marbles were 'an integral part' of the British Museum and would remain. Members of the Greek and British Committees for the Restitution of the Parthenon Marbles have, nevertheless, stepped up their campaign, in the hope that the Marbles will be returned to Greece prior to the Olympic Games, which will be held there in 2004. In January 1999 they won the support of the European Parliament, which voted in favour of a declaration urging the return of the Marbles to Greece. Summer tourists to the Acropolis have also been handed a pamphlet entitled 'The Parthenon Marbles in Exile', which urges them to support the restitution campaign. To my mind, the restitution arguments in this particular case are stronger than those which favour retention. However, as David Lowenthal has wryly commented, 'It may better serve Greek pride to go on demanding the return of the Elgin Marbles than actually to get them back' (Lowenthal 1995: 129).

Caring and sharing

Archaeologists and museum curators can no longer assume that the 'archaeological heritage' is their intellectual property, that they are its primary guardians, that other scientists are their sole audience, or that indigenous peoples should become part of their system. Throughout the world, a large and diverse number of people now claim a moral, if not a strictly legal, stake in the material remains of the past. As David Lowenthal says,

2. Owning the archaeological heritage

'History is still mostly written by the winners. But heritage increasingly belongs to the losers' (Lowenthal 1998: 78). It will increasingly be for indigenous peoples, ethnic minorities and newly independent nations to decide whether or not, and on what terms, they wish to share and preserve their cultural property. Archaeologists and museum staff must therefore learn more about the need for cultural sensitivity, consultation, mutuality and compromise in dealing with these people (Merriman & Rightmire 1995: 20; Vitelli 1996a: 18). Recent changes in the working practices of some archaeologists and museum staff have shown that this is possible, and that mutually beneficial results can follow (e.g. Creamer 1990; O'Regan 1990; Zimmerman 1994; Simpson 1996). Archaeologists do not own the material remains of the past; they must now demonstrate that they deserve a share in them.

3

Protecting the
archaeological heritage

If the physical archaeological heritage can be regarded as property that is owned, it can also be regarded as 'stolen', 'looted' and 'plundered', when it is dishonestly taken from a person or place without right or permission and without any intention of returning it. Throughout the world, the vulnerable and non-renewable material remains of the past are increasingly faced by such a threat; ultimately as a consequence of a rising demand for valuable goods by the antiquities trade and collectors (Bator 1982; Chase et al. 1988; Palmer 1995; O'Keefe 1997). This chapter considers the debates surrounding the question of how best to protect those remains from this illegal threat. (The following chapter will then consider the same question, but in relation to 'legal' threats.)

I shall first introduce the human chain along which stolen antiquities flow. Increasingly well-organised gangs of looters are often found at the 'cutting edge' of illegal destruction at archaeological sites. In under-developed regions, these are usually unemployed local farmers, driven by poverty. In drought-stricken and impoverished Mali, for example, expanding groups of peasants have destroyed hundreds of ancient dwelling mounds in the Inner Niger Delta, in search of sculptures of bronze and terracotta and beads, which they then exchange with local art dealers for money, food and caffeine (Dembélé & Van der Waals 1991; Insoll 1993; Brent 1994; Sidibé

1996; Sanogo 1999). In more developed regions, the looters are also generally driven by financial gain, although some may also be private collectors. In England, for example, a 'night-hawker' who had looted a Roman cemetery at Kempston in Bedfordshire explained to a local newspaper, 'It's all about money. I don't give a shit what people think. I can make a fortune from what I find' (Addyman 1995: 168-9). These looters are often organised and exploited by intermediary dealers and traffickers, who sometimes make large profits. They, in turn, are often involved with corrupt officials. In Cambodia, for example, military officials are thought to play an active part in trafficking pieces of sculpture stolen from the ancient monuments of Angkor and Banteay Chhmar (Ciochon & James 1994; Slayman 1999a). The stolen antiquities then make their way across international frontiers to unscrupulous antiquities dealers based in major cities in the West, who may provide them with fabricated documentation, in return for a significant mark-up in price. The objects are then restored and redistributed, along with fakes, to other antiquities dealers and auction houses, where they are sometimes sold for high prices (Watson 1997). The whole process is cloaked in secrecy, by dealers who regard the ownership, origins, history and destination of an artefact as privileged information (Walker Tubb 1995: 257). But Geraldine Norman, an art market newspaper correspondent, estimated in 1990 that, 'eighty per cent of all antiquities that come onto the market have been illegally excavated and smuggled' (Elia 1995: 247). She has also claimed that, 'In twenty years as an art market correspondent, I have never met an antiquities dealer who did not happily handle smuggled goods' (Norman 1995: 143). Private collections and public museums and galleries in Europe, North America and Japan are the ultimate destination for this illicit trade in antiquities. In Belgium, for example, one of the world's largest collections of Malian terracottas was assembled in the 1970s by Count Baudouin de Grunne, the wealthy Mayor of Wezembeek-

Oppem on the outskirts of Brussels, who bought these objects from antiquities dealers in Brussels and Paris (Brent 1994). Scientific laboratories and art historians may then authenticate these collections, and enhance their market value, by producing reports on them (Elia 1993b).

Associated with this illicit trade in antiquities is a variety of interest groups, each maintaining different justifications for its actions and alternative perspectives towards the question of whether and how the archaeological heritage should be protected. Looters generally talk of financial necessity, but some also claim that they are providing a public service in saving antiquities from crowded museum storerooms. This was the view expressed by an Italian *'tomborolo'* (grave-robber): 'So many things are left underground, and if people from the Superintendency find them they put them in crates and leave them in warehouses for 100 years' (Lattanzi 1998: 49). Corrupt officials in developing countries also point to the need to supplement their paltry salaries. Professional dealers and auctioneers, whose livelihoods depend upon the trade of antiquities, naturally favour a free-market approach (Cook 1995: 185). Their primary interests are: 'to have a stock of antiquities for sale without any legal problems attaching to the transaction from the way in which the antiquity was obtained', and to 'avoid adverse publicity arising from possession of antiquities alleged to have been obtained in dubious circumstances' (O'Keefe 1997: 7). They also argue that the preservation and understanding of the past is not helped 'simply to leave things in the ground, where they are subject to decay and damage through economic development or war' (Ede 1995: 214). Private collectors share these views, since 'their primary interest is in having antiquities to collect' (O'Keefe 1997: 8). They see themselves as performing a public service: assembling collections of beautiful objects, saving them for posterity, and loaning or leaving them to public museums (e.g. Chesterman 1991: 539). They also present themselves as connoisseurs of ancient art. Here, 'the influence of the Modern Movement in the Fine Arts with its cult of the art object bereft of intellectual content ... has been pernicious' (Cannon Brookes 1994: 350). This is particularly evident in the case of the looted marble figures from prehistoric sites on the Greek Cycladic islands, which were integrated into modernist collections in the 1960s and 70s, alongside the work of modernist sculptors such as Moore and Modigliani, which echoed their plain and simple forms (Gill & Chippindale 1993; Chippindale & Gill 1995). Traditional art historians have perpetuated such attitudes, in their desire to study the best examples of ancient art of different periods and styles. This explains why, in 1997, the audience of the First Courtauld Debate voted four to one in favour of the motion, 'This house believes that the trade in antiquities is fundamental to the proper study of the past' (Eisenberg 1998). Archaeologists generally take a more purist line. They condemn every aspect of the illicit trade in antiquities: pointing to the widespread and illegal destruction that it inflicts on the archaeological heritage, and the consequent irretrievable loss of contextually-based knowledge about the past (e.g. Renfrew 1995). Most national governments, with the assistance of international agencies, have, for their part, passed various laws and conventions intended to protect and to prevent the illegal export of cultural property deemed to be of national significance. I shall briefly outline some major examples of these laws and conventions, before turning to the debate over their effectiveness and over which interest groups they best serve.

National laws and international conventions

A recent example of a national law relating to the protection of the archaeological heritage is the UK Government's 1997 *Treasure Act* (Bland 1999). This Law replaces the old common law of

Treasure Trove. It is intended to serve both as a mechanism for the public acquisition of ownerless precious objects, and to ensure the reporting, recording and preservation of valuable archaeological remains. It begins with a new definition of 'treasure'. This now includes: all gold and silver objects that are at least 300 years old, have a precious-metal content of at least 10%, and were either accidentally lost or intentionally buried in a grave; all coins from hoards that are at least 300 years old (and that comprise at least ten coins, if they are made of copper alloy); and any objects found in association with them. The Act states that everyone, including archaeologists, must report all finds of 'treasure' to the Coroner for the district in which they have been found, within fourteen days. If a museum wishes to acquire part of or all of the find, the Coroner will then hold an inquest to decide whether or not it is 'treasure'. If the find is declared to be 'treasure', a Treasure Valuation Committee, which consists of independent experts drawn from the antiquities trade, will recommend a market value for it. The acquiring museum will then have to pay this sum to the Department of Culture, which then passes it on as a reward intended to encourage the reporting of 'treasure'. This reward is normally paid in full to the finder, unless they have made a prior agreement with the occupier or landowner to share it, or when they have broken the law or trespassed. Breaches of the law can result in the finders' being fined and even imprisoned, and in their rewards being reduced, forfeited, or given to the occupiers and landowners.

An early example of an international convention intended to prevent the illegal export of cultural property is UNESCO's 1954 (Hague) *Convention on the Protection of Cultural Property in the Event of Armed Conflict* (Merriman 1986: 833-42; Krimgold Fleming 1996). This was ratified by 77 nations, particularly in response to the looting of art treasures by Nazi and Soviet forces during the Second World War. Such cultural property includes 'Priam's Treasure', a collection of Early Bronze Age jewellery and other artefacts, found by the German archaeologist Heinrich Schliemann at Hisarlik in north-west Turkey, and removed by the Soviet Trophy Commission from a bunker in Berlin to the Pushkin Museum in Moscow in 1945, where they still remain, despite German requests for their restitution (Meyer 1993; Norman 1998). The Convention requires that, in occupied territory, wartime combatants protect, preserve and leave *in situ* cultural property that is not being used for military purposes, for the benefit of the inhabitants. It has a separate protocol dealing with arrangements for returning cultural property seized during a conflict. A second protocol, making it more difficult to justify attacks on cultural property on the grounds of 'imperative military necessity', was also signed by 84 nations in 1999 (Kimber 1999: 13).

Another important international example is UNESCO's 1970 *Convention on the Means of Prohibiting and Preventing the Illicit Import, Export and Transfer of Ownership of Cultural Property*. Its aim is to reinforce international solidarity between signatory States, of which there were 81 in 1995, and in particular between 'countries of origin', suffering from the illicit trade in antiquities, and 'destination countries', importing such material (Clément 1995: 39). The central Article 7 announces:

'The States Parties to this Convention undertake':

(a) 'to take the necessary measures, consistent with national legislation, to prevent museums and similar institutions within their territories from acquiring cultural property originating in another State Party which has been illegally exported after entry into force of this Convention, in the States concerned. Whenever possible, to inform a State of origin Party to this Convention of an offer of such cultural property illegally removed from that State after the entry into force of this Convention in both States';

(b) (i) 'to prohibit the import of cultural property stolen from a museum or a religious or secular public monument or similar institution in another State Party of this Convention after the entry into force of this Convention for the States concerned, provided that such property is documented as appertaining to the inventory of that institution';

(b) (ii) 'at the request of the State Party of origin, to take appropriate steps to recover and return any such cultural property imported after the entry into force of this Convention in both States concerned, provided, however, that the requesting State shall pay just compensation to an innocent purchaser or to a person who has valid title to that property.' (ibid.: 49-50)

In 1984, UNESCO asked UNIDROIT, the International Institute for the Unification of Private Law, to work on a number of important issues of private law relating to the illicit traffic in cultural objects, in order to complement and enhance the effectiveness and universality of the 1970 UNESCO Convention. This work eventually resulted in UNIDROIT's (Rome) *Convention on the International Return of Stolen or Illegally Exported Cultural Objects*, which was adopted by a Diplomatic Conference in 1995, and came into effect in 1998 (Gerstenblith 1998; Renfrew 1999: 61-76). Under the terms of the Convention, which explicitly includes illegally excavated objects, one Signatory State may demand the return of stolen cultural property from another Signatory State. In order for this return to take place, a court of the requested State must then establish that:

'the removal of the object from its territory significantly impairs one or more of the following interests':
    (a) 'the physical preservation of the object or of its context';
    (b) 'the integrity of a complex object';
    (c) 'the preservation of information of, for example, a scientific or historical character';

(d) 'the traditional or ritual use of the object by a tribal or indigenous community'
'or establishes that the object is of significant cultural importance for the requesting State'. (O'Keefe 1997: 24)

In some respects, such national laws and international conventions have been effective in terms of directly helping to protect the archaeological heritage. The Treasure Act, for example, does appear to have encouraged finders to report more of their finds (Bland 1999: 25). International legal proceedings taken by States to recover stolen or unlawfully exported items of cultural heritage can also work, and have increased in number since the mid-1980s (O'Keefe 1995: 73). Turkey, in particular, has aggressively and tenaciously pursued its looted antiquities, with reference to its established antiquities laws, in a series of highly effective and well-publicised legal cases (Rose & Acar 1995; Rose 1999). In some cases, such litigation can lead to the successful return of demonstrably stolen antiquities to their dispossessed owners. This happened in the case of the Siva Nataraja bronze statue, which was looted in 1976 from a twelfth-century temple at Parthur village in the state of Tamil Nadu in India (Ghandhi & James 1992; Paterson 1996). Having passed through several hands, it was sold in 1982, under a false provenance, by a London dealer to a Canadian oil company. It was eventually seized by police in 1992, whilst undergoing conservation treatment at the British Museum in London. An English court, which heard evidence from experts in stylistic comparison, metallurgy, statistical analysis, soil analysis and even termite workings, then ruled that it was the same Nataraja bronze that had been found in 1976, and ordered its return to India. This, in due course, happened. In many other cases, similar legal claims have been settled out of court, without blame attached to any parties. This occurred, for example, in the case of the 'Lydian Hoard' (Chippindale 1993: 700-1; Kaye

46

& Main 1995; Rose & Acar 1995: 46-8). In the mid-1960s, a collection of more than 360 antiquities, dated to around the end of sixth century BC (the age of the legendary King Croesus of Lydia), was looted from burial mounds in the Uşak region of west-central Turkey. Although the looters were arrested and prosecuted, and the police recovered some of the objects, many of the finest objects were smuggled out of Turkey to antiquities dealers in Switzerland and New York. These objects were then acquired by the Department of Greek and Roman Art of the Metropolitan Museum of Art in New York, which reportedly paid an estimated $1.5 million for them, between 1966 and 1970. It was only in 1986, after some of the objects had been put on public display, that the Republic of Turkey's Director General of Antiquities and Monuments was able to decide that they were the missing looted objects from the Uşak tombs, and to formally demand their return from the Metropolitan. This request was summarily rejected by the museum, and so, in 1987, the Republic of Turkey filed a lawsuit against the Metropolitan. Six years of legal proceedings followed, during which time Turkey amassed considerable evidence indicating that the Metropolitan's objects had indeed been looted from the Uşak tombs. Fragments of wall paintings, for example, were measured and shown to match gaps in the walls of one tomb. In 1993 a compromise was finally reached between the two parties, as the action approached discovery stage. At this point the museum would have been obliged to reveal the old minutes of its acquisition committee meetings, which noted that some of the museum's staff had originally known that the material had been illegally excavated and smuggled out of Turkey. The Metropolitan Museum agreed to deaccession the collection and return it to Turkey, where it is now displayed in the Museum of Anatolian Civilisations in Ankara. As part of the settlement, the Metropolitan Museum and the Turkish Government included a good faith commitment to co-operate on future archaeological excavations and exhibitions.

National laws and international conventions have also been somewhat effective in terms of indirectly helping to protect the archaeological heritage, by stimulating parallel developments in national legislation and policy-making and in professional practice. Publicity surrounding the 1970 UNESCO Convention, for example, captured national attention in the USA, with reports of the looting and destruction of pre-Colombian monuments in Mesoamerica. As a consequence, the US Senate ratified the Convention in 1972, and finally implemented it in the 1983 *Convention on Cultural Property Implementation Act* (Papageorge Kouroupas 1995: 83). As a consequence of the latter, and following requests from countries of origin, the US has now imposed emergency import restrictions on archaeological remains from the states of El Salvador, Bolivia, Guatamala, Peru and Mali (Hingston 1989: 143-6; Papageorge Kouroupas 1995: 86-7). In order to facilitate the policing of these bans, the countries of origin have provided the US authorities with a catalogue of the kind of objects that are looted from particular areas and illegally exported. The 1970 UNESCO Convention has also stimulated the development of voluntary ethical standards and codes of practice by professional bodies of dealers, museum staff, archaeologists and laboratory staff. The 1987 *Code of Practice for the Control of International Trading in Works of Art*, to which all the major British art dealers are party, states that members,

'undertake, to the best of their ability, not to import, export or transfer the ownership of such objects where they have reasonable cause to believe':

(a) 'the seller has not established good title to the object under the applicable laws'

(b) 'That an imported object has been acquired in or exported from its country of export in violation of that country's laws'

(c) 'That an imported object was acquired dishonestly or illegally from an official excavation site or monuments or originated from an illegal, clandestine or otherwise unofficial site' (O'Keefe 1997: 49-50).

Likewise, the UK Museums Association's 1997 *Code of Conduct for People who Work in Museums* clearly and firmly states that, 'Museums should not accept on loan, acquire, exhibit, or assist the current possessor of, any object that has been acquired in, or exported from, its country of origin (or any intermediate country in which it may have been legally owned) in violation of that country's laws' (Museums Association 1997: 7). Also, the Society of American Archaeology Ethics in Archaeology Committee's 1995 *Principles of Archaeological Ethics* include the statement that, 'As part of the important record of the human cultural past, archaeological materials are not commodities to be exploited for personal enjoyment or profit', and that 'Archaeologists should abstain from any activity that enhances the commercial value of archaeological objects not curated in public institutions, or readily available for scientific study, public interpretation, and display' (Lynott & Wylie 1995: 23). A similar policy was also recently adopted by Oxford University's Committee for Archaeology, following media exposure of its Research Laboratory for Archaeology and the History of Art, which was earning money from the thermoluminescence dating and authentication of looted Mali terracottas, including pieces in the De Grunne collection, whose market values were being enhanced as a result. The Committee passed a resolution pertaining to 'fired clay artefacts of West African origin', stating that, in the future, the Research Laboratory would no longer carry out testing and authentication for private individuals, salerooms or commercial galleries (Chippindale 1991: 6-8;

Inskeep 1992). Some academic journals have also established editorial policies that refuse to publish unprovenanced antiquities. The *American Journal of Archaeology*, the official journal of the Archaeological Institute of America, for example, announced in 1978 that it would 'not serve for the announcement or initial scholarly presentation of any object in a private or public collection acquired after 30 December 1973, unless the object was part of a previously existing collection or has been legally exported from the country of origin' (Cook 1991: 536).

UNESCO itself has also played a leading role in putting the principles of its Conventions into practice. Together with its *List of World Heritage in Danger*, it has co-ordinated a series of international projects designed to enhance the protection of threatened World Heritage Sites (UNESCO 1997). In 1992, for example, UNESCO assisted the Cambodian authorities in developing a plan to safeguard and enhance the ancient monuments of Angkor, by organising a national workshop in Phnom Penh on legislation, site and museum security, export controls by police and customs authorities, the preparation of inventories of cultural goods, education and public information. Internationally, this led to co-operation with organisations such as the International Council of Museums (ICOM), which published a booklet containing descriptions and photographs of 100 objects stolen from Angkor, and INTERPOL, whose assistance resulted in locating some of the missing objects.

There are, however, numerous limitations to all of these national laws and international conventions. This is ultimately demonstrated by the fact that, around the world, the theft of cultural objects is still increasing (Prott 1995: 58).

UNESCO's 1970 Convention has, in particular, been repeatedly criticised, and 'the high hopes and soaring rhetoric' that accompanied its drafting have been deflated (Merriman 1986; Schmidt & McIntosh 1996: 3, 12). National ratification and legal implementation have been major problems. Although many victim countries have ratified it, major art-marketing states have generally declined to do so, with the recent exception of the USA and France (O'Keefe 1997: 23). The same problem applies to the 1954 UNESCO Convention and the 1995 UNIDROIT Convention, neither of which the USA has ratified (Krimgold Fleming 1996; Gerstenblith 1998).

National laws also vary considerably in the degree to which they conform to UNESCO's principles. Here, again, there is a clear contrast between victim nations, which may emphasise the importance of promoting and sustaining the national ownership of national treasures, and market nations, which 'are less prone to attitudes of national property' (Palmer 1995: 26-7). English laws intended to protect cultural property are notoriously limited and permissive. There is, for example, 'no legal prohibition on bringing into England antiquities that have been unlawfully exported from another country' (O'Keefe 1995: 77). English laws represent a compromise between different interest groups, but above all they reflect the political and economic influence of the huge London art market, which imported fine art and antiquities estimated to value £1.45 billion in 1991: 'a golden egg indeed' for the Government's Treasury (Renfrew 1995: xix; Boylan 1995: 94). The UK Government has provided a diversity of reasons for declining to sign up to UNESCO's 1970 Convention and similar European Community Regulations, including the need to enact legislation; the bureaucratic burden of implementing them; the general resource implications; the consequent interference with rights of ownership; and the damage which could be done to the UK's flourishing art trade (e.g. Morrison 1995). It has also been argued that victim countries must take the blame for failing to protect their own property and patrimony, and that professional codes will regulate the market and ensure an increased protection of the archaeological heritage.

But such codes, however well-intentioned, are of limited value, if not 'virtually useless' (Butler 1995: 227). They can only be enforced by and against members of the relevant group or their disciplinary body, and cannot be invoked by dispossessed owners. Instances of action taken against members for breach of the relevant code are very rare. Also, their terms are open to differential interpretations. In the 1987 *Code of Practice for the Control of International Trading in Works of Art*, for example, the use of phrases such as 'to the best of their ability' and 'have reasonable cause to believe' allow considerable latitude to members (O'Keefe 1997: 50). The Museums Association's 1997 *Code of Conduct for People who Work in Museums* has also been accused of being 'better designed to protect the museum from liability in conversion than to marginalise illicit trade as such' (Palmer 1995: 18).

New national laws relating to the protection of the archaeological heritage may be preferable, but they too have their weaknesses. There are often rules specifying that after a certain 'limitation' period no legal proceedings may be commenced to recover stolen goods that have been bought by an innocent purchaser, and in some countries this period is astonishingly short. In England, for example, it is just six years from the date of that 'conversion' (ibid.: 86). National laws also tend not to be retrospective. The US emergency import restrictions on archaeological remains from certain victim states, for example, are prospective only: the 'emphasis is not the recovery of past losses but rather the protection of cultural property that remains in situ in the country of origin' (Papageorge Kouroupas 1995: 85).

Ultimately, laws are 'only as good as their enforceability and the level of compliance which they attract' (Schadla Hall 1996: 12). In Scotland, for example, which is regarded as having a relatively effective Treasure Trove law, problems still remain (Sheridan 1995: 200-1; 1996: 9). A shortage of resources hinders the monitoring of illicit activities at archaeological sites, the undertaking of legal proceedings and the provision of reward money. There is widespread public and professional ignorance and confusion about the law. Non-reporting of finds, and their sale to private collectors and dealers, is also encouraged, both by suspicion that the authorities will not pay the full market value of a find as a reward, and by reluctance on the part of finders to part with 'their' finds. Elsewhere, levels of state funding and the sheer logistics of site protection are major problems. Official neglect and corruption are also widespread. For example, according to a member of the British Police's Arts and Antiques Squad, 'Pakistan has a total ban on the export of its cultural heritage, yet its officials are so easily bought that it makes a nonsense of their law' (Ellis 1995: 224).

Even working within the confines of national laws, international litigation can still work, but only 'where it is relentlessly pursued and where the object is precious enough to justify the investment' (Palmer 1995: 5-6). In practice it is extremely difficult to ensure the return of looted objects to their country of origin. As a British police officer has noted, 'this process is stacked against the loser' (Ellis 1995: 222-3). Looters do not keep records of their activities, yet requesting countries must be able to identify a stolen object, and show when, where and from whom it was stolen, which is extremely difficult to prove. Furthermore, many individuals, institutions and under-developed nations simply do not have the resources to undertake massively expensive legal proceedings in a foreign country, involving intricate questions of fact and law. The case of the 'Sevso Treasure' highlights some of these problems (Hoffman 1994; Renfrew 1999: 31-7). The Marquis of Northampton bought a collection of late Roman silver vessels from dealers, which he later offered for sale through the auctioneers Sotheby's. The collection was then withdrawn from the market, when it became the subject of law-suits filed in New York by Lebanon, Croatia and Hungary, all of whom claimed that the objects had been looted from their territory. The Lebanese government later dropped its claim, since the objects clearly originated from somewhere in Eastern Europe. Croatia and Hungary's claims were supported by meticulous evidence, based upon the laboratory analysis of wood, soil and insect samples. However, the Court decided that neither Croatia nor Hungary was able to carry the burden of clearly proving that the 'treasure' had been excavated within their respective borders. The Sevso Treasure was therefore left in the hands of the Marquis of Northampton, but without establishing his clear legal title to it.

Changing attitudes

There are no easy ways forward. However, increasingly it is being realised that legislation, although it does help to protect the archaeological heritage from illicit threats, may not be the ultimate solution to the problem of the looting and trafficking of antiquities (e.g. Papageorge Kouroupas 1995: 89; Brent 1996: 75). Changing public attitudes, and enhancing public concern and involvement, may provide an important longer-term alternative.

Colin Renfrew, head of the Illicit Antiquities Research Centre based at Cambridge University, argues that concerned groups must work towards the moral shaming of the collectors and dealers of looted antiquities, and must encourage visitors to museums and galleries to believe that it is no longer acceptable publicly to display antiquities that are either clearly looted or lack a proper provenance (Renfrew 1995: xx-xxi). (Native Americans, of course, have argued this for some time (White Deer 1997: 40).) Renfrew forcefully expressed this view in relation to the private collection of antiquities belonging to George Ortiz, which was shown at the Royal Academy in London. He publicly stated that, 'It is our job to collectively deprecate this, and to ensure that Mr Ortiz goes away a little more ashamed than when he came since he is doing the past great damage by financing the large scale looting which is the ultimate source of so much of what he is able to exhibit' (Renfrew 1995: xxi).

This is not to say that there should be a total ban on the antiquities trade, for some artefacts have been legally excavated and exported, having come either from old excavations or from recent excavations which still result in a share of the finds with foreign collaborators. However, supplies of such 'licit' antiquities are limited and dwindling. A premium should therefore be placed on well-documented objects which come onto the market, in contrast to unprovenanced objects which should become less profitable and thus less attractive (Cannon Brookes 1994: 350).

At the other end of the trafficking chain, collaboration with and re-education of potential looters may prove to be a particularly positive long-term strategy. Archaeologists must begin by trying to bridge the gap between themselves and local people. In the Italian region of Tuscany, for example, many residents see archaeologists as total outsiders with little concern for their local heritage, who take their best finds away with them and do little to share their results, and so they naturally reciprocate by keeping their discoveries to themselves (Thoden van Velzen 1996). Elsewhere, new collaborative projects are paying dividends. In the East Anglia region of England, for example, collaboration between archaeologists and metal detectorists has led to the reporting and accurate recording of large numbers of archaeological finds by members of the public, including the 'Hoxne Hoard' of more than 14,000 late Roman coins, which careful archaeological investigations were able to show had been buried in a wooden container (Addyman 1995: 167; Sheldon 1995: 177-9). This collaborative approach was recently endorsed by the Government's Department of Culture, which funded pilot schemes of finds liaison officers to promote the voluntary recording of archaeological objects by members of the public, which has in turn led to a doubling of the number of finds being recorded (Spencer 1998: 20-1; Bland 1999: 26). Similarly, in the village of Agua Blanca in Ecuador, internationally funded research directed by Colin McEwan has succeeded in transforming local *'huaqueros'* (looters) into enthusiastic archaeologists: by incorporating them in his archaeological excavations and plans for a local museum, which has in turn given them a greater empathy for, understanding of and pride in their cultural heritage (Howell 1996). Ultimately, incorporating potential looters into the heritage process makes good sense in terms of protecting the physical archaeological heritage.

4

Managing the archaeological heritage

Illegal activities certainly pose one of the greatest threats to the world's archaeological heritage. But we should not overlook the fact that a diversity of 'legal' activities also exerts competing demands upon archaeological resources, which may threaten their physical and cultural integrity. This kind of destruction is occurring at a particularly alarming rate in intensively developed parts of the world. In England, for example, around 23,500 ancient monuments have been lost in the fifty-year period since 1945, at a rate of one monument per day (Darvill & Fulton 1998: 6).

'Legal' threats come from a diversity of sources and raise numerous conflicts of interest. In West Germany and England, the most common threats to be listed by archaeologists are building, civil engineering, raw material extraction, agriculture, forestry, military training, visitor erosion and natural processes (Reichstein 1984: 38; Darvill & Fulton 1998: 6-7). Clashes of interest are equally varied and are sometimes also extremely complex. In Hawaii, for example, disputes over the preservation of archaeological sites have occurred: between archaeologists, on the one hand, and Native Hawaiian activists and environmental organisations, on the other hand; between Native Hawaiian activists and the US Navy; between archaeologists and developers; between archaeologists and government agencies; and between different teams of archaeologists, working for different interest groups (Spriggs 1990).

Before turning to some key contemporary debates surrounding the management of the archaeological heritage, it is worth examining in some more detail such threats to the archaeological heritage, and their associated conflicts of interest.

In urban areas, property development and urban expansion have been both destructive and controversial. Developers, on the one hand, argue that, 'there has rarely been a time like the present when new development has been so necessary' (McGill 1995: xvii). Conservationists, on the other hand, have vociferously argued that the archaeological heritage is a finite resource that is rapidly diminishing due to development. Battles between these two groups have been particularly intense in Beirut, the capital city of Lebanon, which is undergoing a process of post-war reconstruction and development (Naccache 1998). Since 1994, the city's inhabitants and political opposition movements have protested, with limited effect, at the bulldozing of large sections of the rich archaeological and architectural heritage of the city centre, with little or no archaeological study, by the employees of a private real-estate company called 'Solidere'. This company, whose 'father' was the Prime Minister, Rafic Hariri, has enjoyed the full backing of the Lebanese state, and the participation of Lebanese and European salvage archaeologists working under UNESCO's supervision.

In rural areas, mechanised farming techniques and agricultural intensification have been equally destructive. This is particularly evident in Western Europe, where the Common Agricultural Policy, used to stimulate agricultural production, 'has had an indirect but tremendous negative influence on the survival of archaeological remains' (Willems 1998: 300). In the Netherlands, for example, it has been estimated that 33% of the archaeological remains surviving in the soil in 1945 had disappeared by 1994, of which 23% was due to intensification of agriculture. The techniques of deep ploughing and land levelling, used both on existing arable land and on previously unploughed areas, have been especially destructive (Lambrick 1977; Harrington 1991). This is obvious to archaeologists but is not widely appreciated by farmers.

Landowners sometimes also choose to exploit the archaeological resources that comprise part of their property for commercial gain. In the USA, for example, Native American Mississippian burials and settlement sites have often been exploited by private property owners, in accordance with property laws which generally allow them to possess and sell anything found under the soil on their land (Harrington 1991). At Slack Farm, near Uniontown in Kentucky, for example, ten professional 'pot-hunters' paid the landowner $10,000 in 1987 for the right to 'excavate' a large Late Mississippian settlement, dated to between the fifteenth and seventeenth centuries AD (Fagan 1988). For two months, they bulldozed their way through the village midden, removing artefacts from more than 700 burials, until local residents finally complained. The Kentucky State police then stepped in and arrested the diggers under a state law that prohibits desecrating a venerated object, such as a human grave. However, in a contrasting example from the Canadian island of St Lawrence, in Alaska, it has been the native Eskimo population that has exploited its archaeological heritage as a much needed source of income (Scott 1984; Staley 1993). Here, the Yupik Eskimo have the legal right to own and administer their own historic resources, under a provision of the 1971 *Alaska Native Claims Settlement Act*. To the dismay of archaeologists who came to study the island, the local Eskimos rapidly learnt that their prehistoric ancestors had left them a large stock of carved ivory artefacts that could be traded for cash. Since then, it has been estimated that during the summer months the exploitation of archaeological sites provides the villagers of Savoonga with about 80% of their cash income.

The construction of major dams and reservoirs has led to the flooding of numerous archaeological sites around the world. The most famous example is the Aswan High Dam in Egypt (Chamberlin 1979: 133-7; Romer & Romer 1993: 116-18). The dam, which was constructed during the 1960s in order to increase the area of Egypt's irrigated land, threatened numerous archaeological sites situated along the Middle Valley of the Nile. These were consequently recorded by an international campaign of rescue archaeology, following a joint appeal by UNESCO and the Egyptian Government. Some monuments, such as the temples of Abu Simbel, were even 'saved' by being moved to higher ground. But, ultimately, the dam led to the creation of an artificial lake of over three hundred miles in length, which flooded the entire land of Nuba and the majority of its archaeological sites. The resultant change to irrigation patterns has also served to permanently soak and weaken the foundations of many ancient Egyptian temples, and to force corrosive salts through their walls.

Military training in archaeologically sensitive areas has also led to the destruction of sites and to conflicts over access. In Hawaii, for example, Native Hawaiian activists mounted a legal campaign in 1976 to stop the US Navy from using Kaho'olawe Island as a bombing range and to have it returned to Native Hawaiians (Spriggs 1990: 123-5). They invoked federal historic preservation laws, and claimed that, 'continued use of live ordnance on Kaho'olawe pollutes the environment, endangers lives, interferes with religious practices and destroys historical sites', and that, in failing to file an environmental impact statement describing the impact of military use of the island, the Navy had violated the National Environmental Protection Act (ibid.: 123). In the end, the activists won the lawsuit. The entire island was placed on the National Register, and the Native Hawaiians were granted monthly access to the island for religious and cultural purposes. However, they failed to get the military use of the island abolished.

Tourists may inadvertently destroy that which they come to see, by bringing with them erosion, pollution, noise and demands for services, such as transport, toilets, entertainment, cafés, souvenir shops and accommodation. In Egypt, where the $3 billion tourist industry is now the country's biggest currency earner, mass tourism has contributed to the gradual destruction of the ancient Egyptian monuments (Romer & Romer 1993). In the Valley of the Kings, for example, millions of tourists have greatly damaged the walls of the Tomb of Seti I by touching and scratching them; vibrations and diesel exhaust fumes from tour buses have accelerated damage in tombs located close to the road; and sewage water leaking from the septic tank of the old Rest House found its way into the Kings Valley 5 Tomb.

Similarly, members of religious groups have sometimes damaged or threatened to damage the objects of their veneration. In England, for example, the National Trust, the official guardians of the phallic Cerne Abbas Giant monument, publicly appealed to childless couples not to make love on it because of fears that it would be damaged, following claims by a woman that she became pregnant by her husband after a nocturnal 'love-in' ceremony on the site (O'Neill 1998b)!

Restorers can also damage the ancient sites and monuments that they seek to return to their original states, by imposing their own images of the past onto its material remains (Stanley Price 1990; Schmidt 1997). A controversial example concerns the Parthenon Marbles, which, as we have seen, were 'cleaned' in 1938 on the orders of Sir Joseph Duveen, a wealthy benefactor to the British Museum, who mistakenly imagined that Classical sculptures would originally have been as white as the more recent plaster casts of them (St Clair 1998; Reynolds 1999). Duveen's workmen attempted to transform the Marbles from brown to white, by scraping them with copper tools and abrasive carborundum, but managed to damage them irretrievably by destroying much of their original surfaces and ancient patina.

Archaeological investigation, however carefully controlled and recorded, must also be recognised as a fundamentally destructive process (Lynott & Wylie 1995: 30). John and Elizabeth Romer specifically point the finger of blame at uncaring Egyptologists for much of the recent damage caused to the Royal Tombs at Luxor (Romer & Romer 1993). In the Tomb of Seti I, for example, the gradual twisting of the tomb, and the cracking and collapse of its famous wall decorations, has been directly linked to the archaeological excavation of wet flood debris from a corridor in the tomb in 1960, which has since served to dry and desiccate the rock in which the tomb is cut.

In these problematic circumstances, the archaeological heritage requires not only active protection, but also effective management. But this raises some familiar questions: How should the material remains of the past be evaluated? How should they be managed? Who has the right to manage them? And for whom should they be managed? The previous chapters have already considered aspects of these questions. Below, I shall introduce three additional areas of contemporary debate that relate to them: the universality of archaeological principles of preservation and conservation; the extent to which the archaeological heritage should be exploited commercially; and the ways in which sacred sites should be managed.

Preserving the past

Archaeologists generally believe in the 'conservation ethic' (Fowler 1982: 20). In other words, they argue that the archaeological heritage is a limited and threatened resource, which should, as far as possible, be managed in such a way that it is protected and preserved for future generations – of scholars in particular. This perspective is clearly reflected in the terms of various international conventions and charters relating to the protection of the archaeological heritage.

One of the earliest and most durable examples is the International Committee on Monuments and Sites (ICOMOS) 1965 (Venice) *International Charter for the Conservation and Restoration of Monuments and Sites*. This codifies the internationally accepted standards of conservation practice relating to buildings and sites. Its principles are based on the ideals of authenticity and of maintaining the historical and physical context of a building or site. The *Venice Charter* has also been influential on a national level. In the UK, for example, it is complemented by the United Kingdom Institute for Conservation's (UKIC) 1983 *Guidance for Conservation Practice*, which defines the responsibilities of conservators in relation to the care and treatment of objects. These documents recognise the fact that material remains are inevitably transformed by undergoing archaeological investigation and conservation, and therefore emphasise four key principles (Stanley Price 1990). (1) Minimal intervention: i.e. that, whenever possible, conservation treatment should aim to preserve the 'true nature' of an object, including its appearance and evidence of its origin, construction and materials, without being invasive or subtractive. In practice, this means that conservators are expected to clean and to stabilise the object so that it holds as it was found. (2) Reversibility: i.e. that all conservation treatment and materials should be reversible. They should not render impossible any different treatment in the future. (3) Compatibility: i.e. that modern conservation materials introduced should be compatible with the original materials, and merge well with them under expected environmental conditions. (4) Documentation: i.e. that meticulous written and photographic records should be kept of all of the stages of conservation treatment that a piece undergoes.

These principles of archaeological conservation were mainly developed in Europe, but have increasingly been applied world-wide. In Athens, for example, the impressive work carried out since the mid-1980s by the Committee for the Conservation of the Acropolis Monuments, has been in accordance with the *Venice Charter* (St Clair 1998: 330). Furthermore, part of the project has involved rectifying the 'errors' made by earlier generations of restorers at the monuments. The same is true of the latest phase of conservation work on the Great Sphinx at Giza in Egypt, carried out since 1989 by the Egyptian Antiquities Organisation in collaboration with an international team of scientists, including the Getty Conservation Institute based in the USA (Hawass 1998). One of the basic principles guiding this work has been the widespread acceptance that, 'The Great Sphinx of Giza is a ruin and should be kept as it is', and that, 'To alter the visual context of the Sphinx is to compromise its original aesthetic excellence, its value as a research subject, and its impact on popular culture' (ibid.: 9). In line with this new approach, Egyptian scholars have also been receptive to criticism of their previous attempts to conserve and restore the monument, which culminated in 1988 in the collapse of a three-ton chunk of rock from the south shoulder of the Sphinx.

Following the *Venice Charter*, successive international recommendations have continued to emphasise the importance of preserving the archaeological heritage. The 1972 UNESCO *Convention Concerning the Protection of the World Cultural and Natural Heritage* invites UNESCO member states to nominate places of 'outstanding universal value' as World Heritage Sites to be included in the prestigious World Heritage List. Such designation has consequently proved effective in strengthening the protection of selected sites. In Mali, for example, local pride in the archaeological heritage has been bolstered by placing the major sites of Jenne and Jenne-jeno on the World Heritage List, which has in turn led to a considerable reduction in clandestine excavations at those sites (O'Keefe 1997: 92). More recently, the ICOMOS International Committee on Archaeological Heritage Management (ICAHM) 1990 *Charter for the Protection and Management of the Archaeological Heritage* has established a new set of international principles and guidelines (Elia 1993a). Its introduction highlights the importance of protecting and managing the archaeological heritage, for present and future generations, through 'the cooperation of government authorities, academic researchers, private and public enterprise, and the general public' (ibid.: 98). It then claims that 'General survey of archaeological resources is ... an essential working tool in developing strategies for the protection of the archaeological heritage' (ibid.: 99). It emphasises that 'the gathering of information about the archaeological heritage should not destroy any more archaeological evidence than is necessary for the protectional or scientific objectives of the investigation' (ibid.: 99). It also recommends that 'Policies for the protection of the archaeological heritage should constitute an integral component of policies relating to land use, development and planning as well as of cultural, environmental and educational policies' (ibid.: 98). This latter suggestion has been matched recently by the Council of Europe's *Recommendation on Cultural Landscape Areas*, which urges member states to incorporate policies for the conservation of the cultural landscape within their general landscape policies (Fairclough 1999: 126).

These recommendations concerning the integration of archaeological heritage management strategies into broader land-use planning policies have now begun to be put into practice in a number of parts of Europe. This is particularly the case with environmental impact assessments of rural landscapes, in which the archaeological heritage is now usually regarded as one of the 'givens' in landscape considerations (Fowler 1995;

Willems 1998). Indeed, a significant degree of complementarity is now recognised as existing between the management needs of archaeological heritage managers and nature conservators. Archaeological heritage managers in the UK have been at the forefront of some of these developments. English Heritage, for example, in their landscape assessment of Hadrian's Wall, the Roman period World Heritage Site in Northumbria, has worked together with the Countryside Commission in developing a wider and more flexible approach to the landscape, which integrates its historic character with the needs of tourism and conservation values that highlight its ecology and scenery (Fairclough 1999; Young 1999). The UK Government's Environmentally Sensitive Areas (ESA) scheme, designated under the 1986 *Agriculture Act*, also encourages the integration of conservation objectives, including the protection of archaeological sites, within 'alternative' farm management schemes (Macinnes 1990; 1993). At the same time, many archaeologists have begun to share the ideals of 'green' activists, and have joined them in highlighting the extent and significance of on-going changes and damage to the countryside (e.g. Barber & Welsh 1992; Pitts 1992; McGlade 1999: 458-9). In 1996, for example, the Council for British Archaeology joined five environmental groups, including Friends of the Earth, Greenpeace, the Royal Society for the Protection of Birds, the Wildlife Trusts and the World Wide Fund for Nature, in protesting at plans submitted by the Highways Agency and Newbury District Council for the new road to bypass Newbury, which threatened to damage twelve archaeological sites as well as an environmentally precious landscape (Clover 1996).

There are, however, some cases where the international principle of archaeological preservation has been taken to the extreme. In the USA, for example, the Archaeological Conservancy was founded in 1979 as a private organisation, with the aim of ensuring the permanent protection of archaeological sites on private land by purchasing those sites and maintaining them for the public on a permanent basis (McGimsey & Davis 1984: 123; Fagan 1995a). In the first fourteen years of its existence, the Archaeological Conservancy acquired 100 archaeological sites in twenty-two States, including the Hopewell Mounds Group in Ohio, which was later developed into the Hopewell Culture National Historical Park. In the English region of Derbyshire, heritage managers took the principle of archaeological preservation even further when they decided to preserve the Gardom's Edge prehistoric cup-and-ring marked stone from further erosion by burying it in a secret location and by erecting a replica on its site (Walster 1996). In 1996, the original stone was buried in soil, covered with a geotextile sheet, and hidden under a layer of soil. The replica was then mounted in an area adjacent to, rather than above, the original – contrary to information provided to the public. As a member of the project stated, 'The re-burial of the original rock was a difficult ethical decision to make, but the process is at least reversible should ideas change in the future'(ibid.: 37). Whether or not all archaeologists would agree with the decisions taken in this particular project, there is at least widespread archaeological agreement on the fundamental principles of preservation and conservation.

This belief is, however, being questioned, as is the associated current Western obsession with conservation. Reversibility in the conservation process, for example, appears to be an impossible aim (Corfield 1988). Conservationists sometimes forget that the physical transformation and decay of the material remains of the past is a natural process (Bradley 1994). Some commentators are even arguing that selective discard needs to be recognised as an integral part of the heritage process (e.g. Ascherson 1999). Such views are now being expressed, to varying degrees, by post-colonial heritage managers, religious groups, local peoples and even by conservators and museum curators.

Post-colonial heritage managers in Zimbabwe, for example, have explicitly rejected a purely conservation-led approach to the protection, restoration and management of the World Heritage Site of Great Zimbabwe (Ndoro 1995; Pwiti 1995). During the period of British colonial rule in 'Rhodesia', this large Iron Age settlement site was investigated, interpreted and restored without reference to the indigenous local people, either living or dead. However, after Zimbabwe gained its independence in 1980, the site was adopted as a national symbol: in name, and physically as a National Monument. Furthermore, under a new political policy, which emphasised the principle that local people should not be alienated from their past, post-colonial heritage managers began to seek the active involvement of local communities in the management of the site. Some local traditional leaders argued against any interference at the site, which they regard as the home of their ancestors and as a religious centre. They believe that there is nothing amiss with the process of disintegration, and that this simply reflects a natural process in which the ancestors abandon their homes and relocate to some other place. Conservation concerns were also rejected by some politicians, who ruled that two large trees, which grow within and threaten the walls of the Great Enclosure, could not be removed, since they are represented on Zimbabwe currency and elsewhere as a national symbol. As a consequence, heritage managers at the site have argued that 'although the principles of conservation may be universal, intervention at each ruined structure or site depends on the local circumstances. The solution must arise out of the ethos and social environment of the particular culture we are seeking to conserve' (Ndoro 1995: 92). This approach has underlain the major restoration works carried out on the collapsing dry-stone walls at the site since 1986. Instead of introducing new materials, expensive equipment and high-level technical expertise, which had been recommended by a joint project between the University of Zimbabwe and the English University of Loughborough, the site's managers have restored sections of the drystone walling by employing local labourers to simply use the same materials and techniques as the original builders. At the same time, local people have acted as custodians of the site, stopping tourists from climbing on the walls, for instance.

New Age religious groups and local people in the English region of Norfolk have also reacted strongly against archaeological conservation concerns in the case of 'Seahenge' (Miles 1999a; 1999b; Purves 1999; Wainwright 1999). In 1998, a Bronze Age enclosure, formed by a circle of vertically-set timbers surrounding the inverted bole of an oak tree, was exposed by erosion at Holme-next-the-Sea on the Norfolk coast. Archaeologists immediately recognised it as an important discovery, and as a valuable potential source of information about the Bronze Age. Therefore, given the threats posed to the monument by further maritime erosion, and to the environmentally sensitive landscape within which it lay by increasing visitor numbers, archaeologists working on behalf of English Heritage decided to excavate the site and to 'rescue' the wooden structure. This decision was taken 'after careful consideration and consultation' with English Heritage's own scientists, marine specialists at Portsmouth and Newcastle Universities, English Nature, the Norfolk Wildlife Trust and Norfolk County Council's archaeologists. The decision invoked an angry reaction from a New Age alliance of Druids, neo-pagans and eco-warriors, who protested at the brutality and 'sacrilege' of damaging and digging up a sacred site, arguing that the monument should be left *in situ* and allowed a 'natural death'. One of the protesters claimed that, 'English Heritage are vandals, destroying our culture' (Wainwright 1999). Local people joined the protest, expressing their bitterness and sense of violation at the thought of their new-found local heritage being taken away from them, and at not having been properly consulted by English Heritage. The archaeologists were clearly surprised by the passion that their decision had aroused, and English Heritage's chief archaeologist, David Miles, tried to reason with the protestors, arguing that, 'The protestors have got the wrong idea. We would dearly love to leave the circle where it is, but if we did it would be destroyed. .... We have to take the timbers away and preserve them' (ibid.). After having applied for, and won, court injunctions to ban the protestors from interfering with the work of the archaeologists, English Heritage used a mechanical digger to extract the timbers, which were then transported to Flag Fen, an archaeological heritage centre which specialises in preserving waterlogged prehistoric wood. In this case, it would apear that the archaeologists 'won' and the protestors 'lost', but the conflict between them certainly generated much public debate about the principle of archaeological preservation and about the right of archaeologists to invoke it.

A similar debate has also been going on in museums in Britain over their retention of large archaeological excavation archives (Pearce 1990: 74-7; Swain 1997a; 1997b; Merriman & Swain 1999). The latter include often-considerable samples of environmental remains, animal bones, building materials and artefacts. Archaeologists have always assumed that the rightful places for their excavation archives are museums, which would permanently store, care for and provide access to them, at no further cost to the archaeologist or developer; and museum curators have generally accepted this responsibility. However, many museums now find themselves under considerable pressure, both as a result of the last thirty years of rescue archaeology, which has filled their storage facilities to bursting point, and as a result of inadequate funding for maintaining museum stores. According to a national survey carried out by the Society of Museum Archaeologists, 'Most museums have run out, or are rapidly running out, of storage space for archaeological material', and 'Museum budgets are not growing to cope with these increases' (Swain 1997b: 2).

The responses of professional museum staff to this situation have been varied. Some museums have taken, or are considering, extreme action. In 1996, for example, the former Director of the Museum of London, Max Hebditch, closed the museum's archive in response to a cut in funding, which forced London's archaeological units and commercial contractors to store their own finds, under the guidance of English Heritage, until the archive was re-opened in 1998 (Swain 1997a: 122; Thomas 1998: 9). Other museums have introduced storage charges for the long-term storage of excavation archives, payable by the developer on deposition of the archive at the museum (Owen 1996: 37). Some curators have even called for the selection of new, and the disposal of old, archaeological material as a last resort. Another response to these problems has been for bodies of museum professionals to encourage their members to establish formal collecting policies, with particular reference to acquisitions and disposals. The 1997 Museums Association *Code of Conduct for People who Work in Museums*, for example, states that 'A museum should collect within a collections management policy that addresses issues of acquisition, public access, collection care and disposal. The policy should relate to the museum's existing collection, fundamental purpose and aims. ... It should lay down the criteria for future acquisitions, including the subjects or themes and the time periods and geographical areas' (Museums Association 1997: 8).

Commodifying the past

Another set of debates relating to the management of the archaeological heritage surrounds the economic exploitation of the material remains of the past. From a commercial perspective, the archaeological heritage can be valued and managed as an economic resource, which has the potential to generate much needed income and employment. But, according to certain archaeologists, this process should be frowned upon, since it leads to the devaluation of the archaeological heritage and of archaeological research. There are many arguments for and against these points of view.

Much can be said in favour of the management of selected archaeological sites and their associated museums and heritage centres as foci for global cultural tourism. From an archaeological point of view, their designation as national and international heritage sites often stimulates efforts to protect and preserve them in the face of modern developments. And from an economic point of view, they can attract large numbers of tourists, who often contribute to the economic development of impoverished regions, by generating income and local employment, and by encouraging private, public and international investment.

An early example of 'tourist archaeology' was Chile's Easter Island in Polynesia (Rapu 1990). In 1966, the Chilean government, with the support of UNESCO and the (then) International Fund for Monuments, recognised that the island's prehistoric monuments were its most important economic resource, and agreed to develop the whole island as a profitable open-air museum. As a consequence, the archaeological monuments were conserved and restored, the administrative status of the island was improved, and funding was provided for the construction of an airport, a new school and facilities for several public services.

Britain has also come to rely on its historical and archaeological sites to generate tourist income. In the Scottish Highlands, for example, some ten new archaeology- or history-oriented heritage centre projects were developed in the first half of the 1990s, to profit from the estimated 2.04 million tourist visits per year to the Highlands and Islands (Hanley 1996). All except one of these centres charge for admission, and the majority are run as independent trusts, receiving grant-aid from sources including local government, the Scottish Museums Council and economic development agencies. As a consequence, these centres have, directly and indirectly, led to the creation of new jobs in often-isolated rural communities.

Such projects can also have a commercial impact on a much broader scale. At Çatalhöyük in Turkey, for example, renewed archaeological work at the Neolithic settlement, whose material culture is famous for its decorated walls and 'Mother Goddess' figurines, has stimulated numerous commercial interests (Hodder 1998). Locally, the archaeological project has brought money into the region and increased employment. Regionally, carpet dealers in Konya have begun to use designs from Çatalhöyük in order to enhance their sales. Nationally, an Istanbul-based PR firm and its parent credit-card company, which sponsors the project, hand out replicas of a 'Mother Goddess' figurine with the company name on it to their clients at receptions in Istanbul. And internationally, travel agencies in Istanbul, Britain and the USA vie with each other to organise special-interest packages for Californian Goddess tourists.

Another set of arguments can be made in favour of professional archaeologists seeking to make profits from their work. Archaeologists, it is said, need to embrace the concept of profit, for 'profit is what enables commercial companies to weather temporary lulls in their markets, to research and develop new ideas, to improve working practice and standards, and to allow for capital investment' (Lawson 1993: 157). The privatisation of groups of professional archaeologists, the development of competition between them and the assessment of their work in terms of value-for-money, are also justified in similar economic terms, and are regarded as an inevitable consequence of working within a Western capitalist economy.

In Britain, for example, an increasingly commercialised

system of 'contract archaeology' has been growing since the late 1980s, when private developer funding of archaeological projects replaced public funding as the norm (Swain 1997a). Within this system, self-financing archaeological field units have increasingly competed for excavation work throughout the country, based upon the principles of privatisation of public services, competitive tendering, profit and value-for-money. They have also learnt to liase and collaborate with planners and developers. The York Archaeological Trust, for example, established close relations with the city's planning department and construction agents, and was consequently given long advance warning of redevelopment programmes in the city (Jones 1984: 135). This system was formalised by the Government's Department of the Environment in 1990, with their publication of *Planning and Policy Guidance Note 16: Archaeology and Planning* (PPG16). This document confirms the national importance of the archaeological heritage as a resource, and recommends methods to 'mitigate' its destruction by development projects. Following the 'polluter pays' concept, responsibility is placed on the developer: to ensure that any planning application is accompanied by a detailed statement of archaeological implications, and to pay for professional archaeologists to excavate any archaeological remains that are found.

Despite such economic benefits for archaeologists and others, and the apparent added protection provided for the material remains of the past, the commercial exploitation of the archaeological heritage has also been strongly criticised, particularly by those archaeologists who have traditionally not sought to make profits from their work. They have put forward a variety of arguments. (1) The economic exploitation of archaeological remains often results in physical damage being caused to them (Lipe 1984: 8). (2) As tourist centres, visually impressive, large-scale, masonry constructions are prioritised and preserved at the expense of more ephemeral archaeological sites (Silberman

1995: 259). (3) The establishment of archaeological 'parks' and 'reserves', and their packaging for tourist consumption, is leading to the separation of historical parts of the landscape from the wider context of the living landscape, and to an arresting of the social and economic development of those people who live in them (Cleere 1995: 67; McGlade 1999). (4) The commodification of the archaeological heritage can lead to a fragmentation, de-contextualisation and trivialisation of interpretations of the past, 'in which histories or prehistories do not mean anything other than nostalgia, fun, thrill, excitement' (Hodder 1993: 17). (5) The current level of archaeological heritage centre development is not sustainable, particularly within the context of an already saturated market for heritage attractions in certain parts of the world, where most new centres generate a large proportion of their income through admission charges (Hanley 1996: 58). (6) Developer-funded contract archaeology leads to a lowering of standards of professional practice. In the USA, for example, where contract archaeology is now well established, 'There have been accusations of shoddy work by inexperienced people, of cutting costs to become a low bidder or inflating costs to make a profit, and preparing written reports that contain no real hard scientific data' (McGimsey & Davis 1984: 122). (7) Too much power over the archaeological heritage is placed in the hands of developers. These people, who inevitably choose the cheapest tender, are, 'arguably those who traditionally have had least interest in what archaeology delivers' (Morris 1995: 4). They, consequently, favour the basic recording of archaeological remains, as opposed to their investigation and interpretation within a framework of archaeological research. (8) Many field archaeologists now have to put up with poor employment security and conditions (Barrett 1995: 2). (9) Archaeological excavations are prioritised over post-excavation work. In Britain, for example, PPG16 is inexplicit on the question of who should pay for the publication of excavation reports,

the conservation of finds and the long-term storage of archaeological archives (Swain 1997a: 124-6). (10) Local people have
less opportunities to get involved with archaeological fieldwork,
and to hear about the results of local excavations, particularly
when fieldwork is carried out by a non-local unit (Hawkes
1998). Taken together, these arguments present a serious critique of the contemporary commodification of the
archaeological heritage (cf. Tilley 1989).

In response to the problems raised by such debates surrounding the commodification of the past and the commercialisation
of professional archaeology, various authorities have established more explicit policies. On an international level, the
Council of Europe's 1992 (Malta) *European Convention on the
Protection of the Archaeological Heritage* aims to establish minimum standards for the management of the European
archaeological heritage (O'Keefe 1997: 32; Willems 1998).
These include: making professional archaeologists accountable
to the state and to the public for their actions; taking archaeological remains into account in assessments of the impact of
development plans; placing the cost of necessary archaeological
work on those responsible for development projects; and making provisions for the creation of archaeological reserves for the
preservation of material evidence to be studied by later generations. Bodies of professional archaeologists, including
conservators and museum staff, have also developed their own
standards and codes of ethics and conduct. One of the first steps
in this direction was taken by the Society of Professional Archaeologists (SOPA), which was founded in 1976 in the USA
(Jelks 1995; Vitelli 1996b: 253-60). It defined the minimum
requirements in education and experience to be recognised as a
professional archaeologist, it published a *Code of Ethics* and
Standards of Research Performance, it required members to
indicate their agreement to adhere to these principles, and it
instituted a strict procedure for sanctioning members consid-

ered to have violated them. Similar professional standards and ethics have been adopted by the Institute of Field Archaeologists in the UK (Institute of Field Archaeologists 1995: 14-16). At the same time, professional archaeologists are increasingly taking out insurance policies, to safeguard themselves in case they inadvertently default on their obligations to their clients, employees or the public (Lawson 1993: 157).

Managing sacred sites

Debates surrounding the management of ancient objects, sites and landscapes that are considered to be sacred by particular religious groups highlight fundamental contrasts in the ways that different groups value the archaeological heritage. Within Western culture, ancient physical remains are generally valued highly as 'archaeological' resources, produced by *past* societies, which should be preserved and exploited in the present for purposes such as: historical education, tourism and national identity. But according to the beliefs of many indigenous peoples, it is the ongoing spiritual dimension of these often transitory remains that makes them so vital to their religious lives and to their sense of social and individual identity, and, as a consequence, worthy of special treatment (Carmichael et al. 1994; Ucko 1994). Many Western New Age religious groups have adopted similar belief systems, but have also presented problems for indigenous peoples over the issue of access to their sacred sites. Archaeologists, well trained in scepticism, have generally rejected the beliefs of both indigenous and New Age groups as irrelevant and even dangerous, and have therefore rarely considered the special legal, social and physical treatment of sacred remains to be necessary. These conflicting perspectives are highlighted clearly by arguments surrounding the management of Native American sacred sites.

Native Americans argue that, 'many agencies apply an

ethnocentric approach to the management of historic properties that favours western values over Native American values' (Dongoske & Anyon 1997: 195). As a consequence, they are increasingly challenging archaeologists to conduct their work and to help to manage their sites in a manner that respects their legal rights, tribal authority, religious concerns and research interests. That is not to say that it is easy to find a consensus of attitude and opinion within and between Native American groups (Carmichael et al. 1994: 2). But their point is that an attempt to do so should at least be made. And, in general, 'tribes agree that the best management strategy is to leave cultural remains undisturbed' (Swidler & Cohen 1997: 205).

In the late 1980s and early 1990s, for example, Native American groups protested strongly against plans proposed by the United States Forest Service to manage the Bighorn Medicine Wheel and Medicine Mountain, located in the Big Horn mountains of north-western Wyoming (Price 1994). Various Native American tribes have traditionally used these ancient sacred sites for religious vision quests. However, the Forest Service, in line with its policy to promote a multiple use of the area's 'surface resources', put forward plans to develop the Medicine Wheel as a tourist attraction, with an information centre and a viewing platform placed adjacent to the site, as well as a perimeter fence, walking trails, historical interpretation panels, a widened road and a parking lot. They did not consult any Native Americans. As a consequence, a pressure group, known as the Medicine Wheel Alliance, was formed to promote the Native American viewpoint. They succeeded in getting the Forest Service to drop its plans for the information centre and viewing platform at the site. They also reached an agreement with the Forest Service, the Advisory Council on Historic Preservation and the Wyoming State Historic Preservation Office, to set aside days for the ceremonial use of the site by traditional practitioners, and for Native American representatives to act as advisors to state and federal forest management agencies.

Native American concerns over the management of their sacred sites were legally recognised in 1992, in amendments made to the *National Historic Preservation Act* (NHPA). Under Section 106, these amendments clearly instruct federal agencies to consult with tribes whenever and wherever any Indian tribe or Native Hawaiian organisation attaches religious and cultural significance to places and properties on federal land or within federally funded or licensed projects. President Clinton reinforced this instruction in 1994, in a memorandum ordering federal departments and agencies to improve relations with tribes. In practice, however, there have been numerous problems in the implementation of this consultation process (Swidler & Cohen 1997). Native Americans have accused some federal agencies of not living up to the letter or spirit of the NHPA, and some regulatory agencies of not consistently enforcing the requirement for federal agencies to consult. As one Native American has said, 'What consultation means is that you are going to tell us what you are going to do' (Brooks 1997: 214). Additional problems are caused by difficulties in contacting the appropriate tribes and their appropriate representatives, the fact that tribes do not necessarily know the precise location of all their archaeological sites, and unresolved land disputes between neighbouring tribes.

In the light of these continuing problems, many American Indian tribes have recently exercised their legal rights to preserve, interpret and manage their own archaeological heritage themselves, particularly under the terms of the 1994 *Tribal Self-Governance Act* (Ravesloot 1997). This law authorises Indian tribes to negotiate annual funding agreements to plan, conduct, consolidate, and administer programmes, services, functions and activities previously administered by federal agencies. This has led to the establishment of Native American cultural centres, historic preservation offices and cultural resource management programs. These employ staff, including some professional archaeologists, to conduct cultural resource inventories, make assessments of National Register eligibility, consult with neighbouring tribes, excavate sites, write reports and curate artefacts and records in their own repositories and museums. The Navajo Nation, for example, employs more than one hundred archaeologists, archaeological aides and technicians, the majority of whom are tribal members, to survey and protect the estimated one million archaeological sites found within the Navajo Indian reservation, in the States of Arizona, New Mexico and Utah (Begay 1997: 162-3; Ferguson et al. 1997: 240).

Managing Stonehenge

In the case of Stonehenge, the prehistoric structure situated in the English county of Wiltshire, all three major issues discussed above – preservation, commodification and sacredness – converge in contemporary debates over the management of this national monument and World Heritage Site (e.g. Golding 1989; Chippindale et al. 1990; Michell 1986; Wainwright 1996; Malone & Stoddart 1998: 731-7; Stone 1999). A great diversity of interest groups is participating in these complex and long-running debates. They include: government offices and agencies; local authorities; international cultural agencies; private companies; archaeological organisations; local landowners, farmers and residents; New Age groups; and other members of the public.

The contemporary debate opened in 1984, when the Chairman of the newly founded English Heritage, Lord Montagu of Beaulieu, noted 'increasing dissatisfaction with the way in which Stonehenge is presented to visitors', and announced plans to 'find and implement a permanent solution' (Bainbridge

1979). English Heritage and the National Trust have consequently joined forces to produce a document called *Stonehenge: the Master Plan*. This highlights four key issues. (1) The reception of visitors and the presentation of the site to them. Provisions for visitors to the site, which number nearly one million a year, are lamentable, and in 1993 were described as 'a national disgrace' by the House of Commons Public Accounts Committee. Current plans for the provision of new visitor facilities include an interpretation centre, educational facilities, catering and retail facilities, footpaths, car parking and a shuttle bus service. (2) The road problem. There are two roads which bring traffic too close to the stones, threatening their preservation and marring their environmental setting: the A303 to the south, and the A344 to the north. It is generally agreed that the A344 should be closed and that the A303 should be diverted. However, debate has surrounded the question of where the A303 should be diverted to: the north, the south, or sunk into a long tunnel beneath the site. (3) The preservation of the archaeological remains and the conservation of its surrounding landscape. The site stands at the centre of over 2,000 hectares of ancient landscape, containing 450 Scheduled Ancient Monuments, and a fragile chalk downland habitat, which provides a home for several important species of flora and fauna. Currently, the site is viewed in isolation from this landscape. However, according to the new management plans, the site will be returned to its downland landscape by the closure of the A344 and the diversion of the A303, the removal of the existing visitor facilities, and the placing of the new visitor facilities some distance away from the stones. The monument will then be reached on foot by the majority of visitors, via a twenty-minute walk, with the exception of elderly and disabled people for whom there will be special arrangements. In this way, it is thought that visitors will be ensured access to the stones, but at a minimal physical and visual cost to the site and its surrounding landscape. (4) The locality. These plans for the site are seen as having wider implications for the locality and its inhabitants, above all in economic terms.

These plans carry with them a high price tag, and recent debates have focused on precisely how much the Government is prepared to spend on the re-development of Stonehenge, and whether or not the value of this site can be reduced simply to the financial (Clover 1998; 1999a; 1999b). In 1997, for example, the Government's Millennium Commission turned down English Heritage's application, submitted together with the National Trust and their preferred private finance partner, the Tussards Group Limited, for funds to develop the Stonehenge Millennium Park via a Private Finance Initiative, estimated at a total cost of £83 million. Then, in 1998, the Prime Minister, Tony Blair, ruled out the building of a three-mile long deep-bored road tunnel to bury the A303, estimated at a cost of £300 million, as too costly. Instead, the Government has backed a plan for a £125 million cut-and-cover road tunnel. This plan has been criticised by an alliance of archaeological, environmental and New Age groups, who claim that the cut-and-cover tunnel will destroy sixteen archaeological sites, leave a scar on the landscape and re-introduce the noise of road traffic to parts of the site. Also, in 1999, the Government, in line with its acceptance of the principle of privatisation, invited commercial bids from private developers to build the visitor centre at Stonehenge. Whether or not Stonehenge will be able to 'pay for itself' in the future remains to be seen.

One other important issue, which has not been highlighted by English Heritage, concerns the New Age groups who demand access to the site, which they regard as a sacred meeting place. Barbara Bender, an anthropologist, has portrayed the conflict between these two interest groups in terms of a struggle between the Establishment and an 'alternative' marginalised minority (Bender 1998). To its designated 'official' custodians,

English Heritage and the National Trust, and their archaeologists, the site of Stonehenge and its landscape are seen as, 'something to be preserved, a museum piece, an artefact, a vital part of our rooted, stable, national identity' (ibid.: 9). But for a small minority Stonehenge is something entirely different: 'a living site, a spiritual centre, an integral part of an alternative life-style' (ibid.: 9). Representatives of the Establishment tend to despise these people, as threatening, unacceptable, 'wierdos'. They publicly reject the 'alternative' theories of the New Agers. They also forcefully restrict their access to the stones and the surrounding landscape, on conservation grounds, at great expense and via an increasingly draconian legal system.

This conflict exploded in 1985, when the authorities' grudging tolerance of the unofficial Free Festival that had been held in the field next to Stonehenge for a decade came to an end (Staunton 1986; Behan 1998; O'Neill 1998a; Fleet 1999). The (then) Historic Buildings and Monuments Commission for England (HBMCE) and the National Trust were granted an injunction banning the festival. Despite this, a group of more than 30,000 free festival-goers tried to make their way to Stonehenge. Their route was blocked by the police, and in the ensuing clash, known as the 'Battle of the Beanfield', much damage was caused to the travellers and to their vehicles. There was a repeat performance in 1988, and in 1994 the police were granted an exclusion order, which established a four-mile exclusion zone around Stonehenge for the period of the summer solstice. In 1998, the authorities finally granted permission to a group of New Age worshippers and local residents to carry out the first summer solstice celebrations at Stonehenge for a decade. However, in 1999, over 400 travellers stormed the site prior to the summer solstice celebrations, and about a dozen of them climbed the stones. One of the latter complained that 'The Druids are trying to say they are the only ones who should be allowed there but we should have just as many rights' (Fleet 1999). Clearly some people still feel excluded from Stonehenge.

Local interests

In all of these debates surrounding the protection and management of the archaeological heritage, a standard 'official' response has been to establish new guidelines for professional practice, via international recommendations, conventions and charters; national laws; and professional codes and standards. In general, these moves towards establishing greater personal and professional responsibility for the protection and management of the archaeological heritage are to be welcomed. They all set high standards that cannot easily be ignored. They encourage collaboration and complementarity between different heritage management organisations. They will also continue to develop in the future, in response to new problems. Amongst European archaeologists, for example, there is a growing need to establish core data standards, and an unambiguous and mutually understandable terminology (Willems 1998). And for museums, there is a need for clear guidelines as to how they wish to receive excavation archives (Goodman & Suenson Taylor 1998: 6).

However, these 'official' responses have their limitations. The international recommendations, in particular, aspire to be universally applicable, but ultimately they reflect Western values (Byrne 1991). In practice, their effects may also vary considerably from country to country. The direct impact of the Council of Europe's 1992 *Malta Convention*, for example, is limited nationally by the degree to which it is taken seriously and ratified by member states; national legislation already in force; levels of available finance to implement and enforce it, particularly in poorer eastern European countries; and the strength of local traditional perceptions and practices relating to the exploitation of archaeological resources (Kolen 1995; Willems 1998). Furthermore, although such proposals are often couched in worthy terms of professional heritage managers acting responsibly on behalf of the public and of future generations, in practice they generally invite little active public participation in the protection and management of the archaeological heritage.

In this way, the 'public' are often simply designated as passive consumers of the past: educated, mobilised, dictated to and even misinformed by the 'authorities', who in reality represent vested interest groups, such as archaeologists, tour operators, developers and politicians (Ucko 1990a: xvii-xviii). The traditional archaeological literature on conservation issues, for example, is characterised by calls to 'educate' the public and to 'mobilise' their support for archaeological preservation and protection (e.g. Lambrick 1977: 32; Cleere 1984: 128; Jones 1984). 'Ignorant' farmers, tourists, New Age groups, children and the media are all seen as key targets for such archaeological proselytising, whose ultimate goal often appears to be to maintain data and funding for more archaeological research.

The interests, values and desires of local people, in particular, are rarely prioritised in plans for the protection and management of the archaeological heritage. As a consequence, local people are often denied the chance to develop meaningful connections with the archaeological heritage that they reside amongst. My sympathies lie, then, with the inhabitants of places such as Holme-next-the Sea in England and Medicine Mountain in the USA, whose valid interests in their local archaeological heritage have been overlooked by outsider archaeologists and government agencies, and who have consequently had to shout to be heard. In the same way, my admiration goes out to post-colonial archaeological heritage managers in places such as Zimbabwe, who have had the courage and conviction to resist the advice of Western scientists and heritage agencies, in favour of the principle that local people should not be alienated from their past.

To my mind, then, it is with greater reference to local peoples' interests that solutions to archaeological heritage management problems should be sought. As Peter Fowler has pointed out, of course archaeologists will want the management of archaeological resources to be 'archaeologically correct', but, 'it simply has to be accepted (and preferably welcomed) that nowadays debate about them will be public and decisions about them will be controversial' (Fowler 1993: 5). Archaeological remains, however insignificant to the archaeologist or heritage manager, will always mean something to someone, and 'Woe betide the archaeological manager who ignores, is ignorant of, or, worse, despises, that interest' (ibid.: 5). Modern archaeological heritage managers must therefore keep in touch with what their constituents think, through person-to-person consultation, so that they can try to predict what they will think and how they will react in the light of any new circumstances. In a similar way, 'archaeological' field projects must also be regarded as ethnographic projects (Solli 1996). Archaeologists, by recognising that they generally arrive as strangers within local communities, and that their activities affect the landscape and the people living in it, will then learn to ask, understand and respect what local residents want of them and for themselves.

A number of contemporary examples show how working with local people makes good sense in practice: both from the point of view of heritage managers, developers and archaeologists, in terms of minimising conflict; and from the perspective of local peoples, in terms of negotiating some control over the future of their heritage. In England, the Norfolk Archaeological Trust has, in their work of preserving archaeological sites and of improving public access to them, been particularly concerned with maintaining a balance between the interests of all parties affected by their projects (Wade Martins 1996; Davies 1998). In the case of the Roman town of Caistor St Edmund, near Norwich, for example, the Trust's plans to manage the site have developed within a climate of sensitivity towards local residents, who do not want their peaceful rural existence disturbed by a large influx of visitors. In the USA, the developer of a proposed golf and country club project at Greenhorn Creek in Angel's Camp, California, displayed similar sensitivity (and business acumen) towards the indigenous Central Sierra Me-Wuk community, by involving them from the outset in plans to develop the property (Fuller 1997). They walked the land together, sharing their different perspectives on it, and they identified the remains of prehistoric sites, which they agreed would be protected and presented to the public in open space with 10-metre buffers around them. As a consequence, the Native Americans became enthusiastic supporters of the project. In the Federal States of Micronesia, on Pohnpei Island, a recent archaeological and cultural resources assessment project run by archaeologists and ethnographers from the University of Oregon also succeeded in carrying out an interactive project with the residents of Salapwuk and Pohnpei (Ayres & Mauricio 1999). The main aim of the project was, 'to develop indigenous and alternative rather than just archaeological constructions of the past for accomplishing historic preservation aims', 'incorporating many voices in order to move towards a more integrative perspective' (ibid.: 318-19). Part of the project involved recording local oral traditions related to specific archaeological sites and natural features that have continuing significance as cultural landmarks. The end result of projects such as these will hopefully be the creation of a more flexible and responsive system of archaeological heritage management, comprised of distinct and diverse local, national and global components (Long 1999).

5

Interpreting the archaeological heritage

Archaeologists have traditionally taken upon themselves the social responsibility to not only manage, but also interpret, the archaeological heritage. In doing so, they have portrayed themselves as scientific experts in the art of understanding the material 'facts' of past societies, in the belief that their work is objective and impartial. But sceptics, including 'critical' archaeologists, are now questioning the interpretative authority of archaeologists. They are recognising the partisan nature of archaeological scholarship, which is continually shaped and modified by contemporary forces, particularly when its results are presented to the public (e.g. Tilley 1989; Ucko 1990a; Bond & Gilliam 1994; Rowlands 1994). Some groups are even beginning to criticise archaeologists' expert knowledge, as impersonal, irrelevant or dangerous. At the same time, a diversity of interest groups are now presenting their own competing interpretations of the material 'evidence' of the past, in accordance with their own ethnic, cultural, sexual, social and political values. Furthermore, all of these interest groups, archaeologists included, have used, unconsciously or consciously, the evidence of the past for their own ends. In this way, their representations of past societies have been used as an expression and as a source of power in the present. Not surprisingly, archaeologists have, until recently, usually denied this political aspect of their work.

These issues concerning the status of different interpretations of the archaeological heritage raise another set of important questions to be debated: Who has the right to interpret the material remains of the past? And is there really a single past? (Ucko 1990a: xix; Carman 1995: 96). Before attempting to answer these questions, I shall examine the interpretative positions adopted by three major interest groups: political rulers, the ruled and 'alternative' groups. Archaeologists, for their part, have found themselves caught up in controversies associated with all three groups, and so their position will be considered throughout.

Rulers' interpretations

Those in power often produce accounts of the past to legitimise their own political positions, to influence present social practices and values and to naturalise the past so that it appears to lead logically to the present (Gathercole 1990a: 1; Gero & Root 1990: 19). In doing so, they have frequently drawn upon selected material remains of the past, and, more specifically, upon the services of archaeologists who have depended upon them for funding. Their interpretations have commonly relied upon a 'culture-historical' approach, based upon the assumption that distinct archaeological assemblages correlate with individual cultural groups (Shennan 1989; Trigger 1989: 148-206). Using this approach, politicians and traditional archaeologists have claimed to trace the origins and movements of those historically documented and modern ethnic and national groups that they have a particular interest in, and their superiority over less favoured populations. In this way, they have used the dubious archaeological evidence of ancient ethnic migrations to legitimise contemporary territorial expansion and ethnic persecution: 'assuring the dominated of their right to rule, and convincing the dominated of their duty to obey' (Miller et al.

1989: 22). Most archaeologists are now highly sceptical of the culture-historical approach, and its 'none-too-subtle ascription of racial/cultural stereotypes to static material culture items' (Ucko 1990a: xi). But its legacy lives on throughout the world: in old textbooks, museums and reconstructions of archaeological sites; and also in contemporary regions characterised by racial oppression and the abuse of human rights. This highly political approach to the interpretation of the archaeological heritage can be loosely divided into various overlapping forms: nationalist, federalist and imperialist/colonialist.

Nationalistic archaeological interpretations are normally promoted by central government agencies and their dependent state-funded archaeologists (Kohl & Fawcett 1995; Trigger 1984; 1995; Díaz Andreu & Champion 1996). They are concerned only with certain kinds of representations of the past, in particular those that tend to emphasise the political and cultural achievements of archaeologically recent complex societies, which can be used to provide simple educational messages about national cultural identity. They function primarily to enhance the identity and bolster the pride of members of nations and their favoured ethnic groups. They may also be used to justify the appropriation of territories claimed to be ancestral, or to support policies of domination over particular groups within society or over neighbouring peoples. The archaeological heritage lends itself well to nationalistic interpretations for a number of reasons. (1) Being ambiguous and versatile, at the same time as inviting interpretation, it lies open to interpretative distortion. (2) Being old and durable, it can be used to supply historical 'evidence' of the origin, antiquity and longevity of a particular group's occupation of a territory. (3) Being physical, it can constitute a source of information for understanding the past that is independent of the written word. (4) Being visually impressive, archaeological sites and monuments can also provide evocative arenas for nationalistic political gatherings and educational visits. Over the past two centuries, no country has been totally free from nationalist influence on archaeological interpretations, although these have varied considerably in content and importance (e.g. Seeden 1990; Díaz Andreu 1995; Fawcett 1995; Kaiser 1995; Guidi 1996). Furthermore, over the past few years, there has even been a certain revival of nationalist archaeology, particularly in regions experiencing ethnic wars associated with the break-up of old regimes and the emergence of new nation-states. Here are three major examples.

In Nazi Germany, the results of archaeological excavations were sometimes actively distorted by politicians and manipulated by certain archaeologists in order to enhance the prehistoric Germanic past and to support the myth of Germanic racial superiority (Arnold 1990; McCann 1990; Arnold & Hassmann 1995; Wiwjorra 1996; Junker 1998). Heinrich Himmler, in particular, made use of archaeologists to obtain pseudo-scientific support for his theories about Atlantis, the Holy Grail and early Germanic symbols, including the swastika that was adopted as the Nazi party's central symbol. In 1935, he founded the 'SS-Ahnenerbe' (Ancestral Inheritance), whose main task was to investigate Germanic 'spiritual prehistory'. They took over the direction of on-going archaeological excavations, and also carried out their own excavations, particularly of Germanic sites, both within Germany and on its eastern borders. Through these, attempts were regularly made to show that either Germans or Germanic tribes were the first settlers to bring civilisation to areas previously inhabited by inferior races. Herbert Jankuhn, a German archaeologist who worked on behalf of the SS, confidently claimed, for example, that,

Among [Indo-European peoples] the Germanic people play a special role, insofar as they can trace their family tree back furthest, further than the Romans, Celts and Slavs.

92

... It is not just that this earliest entry on the stage of history can be proven on the basis of archaeological finds, but also the fact that we can trace back beyond this the roots out of which the organic people of the *Germani* developed in the North of Europe at the end of the Neolithic period. (McCann 1990: 82)

Such views were publicised via a growing number of archaeological journals, films and open-air museums. But that is not to say that all German archaeologists served the Nazi party. As Bettina Arnold has noted of German prehistorians, there were, 'the party-liners; the acquiescent and passive majority; and the critical opposition' (Arnold 1990: 470).

More recently, a new breed of nationalist archaeological interpretations has emerged since the break-up of the former Soviet Union in the mid-1980s (Chernykh 1995; Kohl & Tsetskhladze 1995; Shnirelman 1996). The Caucasus, in particular, is a hot-bed of ethnically-based archaeological distortion, since many of the contemporary leaders of radical nationalist movements in the different republics are also trained archaeologists and ancient historians. Here, for example, the origins of the domestication of crops and animals, of full-scale metallurgy, and of monumental architecture, are variously assigned: 'in that remarkably creative cradle nestled along the western shore of the Caspian (for an Azeri), in the lush foothills of the Great Caucasus and along the Black Sea coast (for a Georgian), or in the fertile Ararat valley of southern Transcaucasia (for an Armenian)' (Kohl & Tsetskhladze 1995: 168).

Federalism is also influencing representations of later prehistory in Europe, which are being used to legitimate the ideal of a unified contemporary Europe (Dietler 1994; Champion 1996; Shore 1996). The politicians of the Council of Europe lie behind much of this, but archaeologists have joined in, particularly out of a desire to obtain lucrative European funding and publicity for their research protects. In 1992, for example, the Council of Europe's *European Convention on the Protection of the Archaeological Heritage* expressed one of its aims as being 'to protect the archaeological heritage as a source of the European collective memory' (Jones & Graves Brown 1996: 13). The archaeological heritage of the Bronze and Iron Ages, which expresses a degree of cultural homogeneity throughout Europe, has lent itself particularly well to this purpose. This might explain why the Council of Europe designated 1995 to be the Year of the Bronze Age. As part of this, the advance publicity for a conference held in Dublin hailed the Bronze Age as 'Europe's first golden age', with reference to the technical and artistic achievements of Bronze Age goldsmiths in Ireland and on the Continent, and to the idea of a former era of peace and harmony in Europe. The material culture of the Iron Age in Europe and historical references to 'the Celts' have also been re-interpreted by politicians and in major exhibitions to emphasise a theme of early European cultural unity and common roots.

Imperialist and colonialist interpretations of the archaeological heritage have also served to promote a sense of racial and cultural superiority, particularly among European and Euro-American peoples, and to justify their military conquest, political subjugation and economic exploitation of native populations (Giridi 1974; Trigger 1984; Trolle Larsen 1989; Rowlands 1989; Gathercole & Lowenthal 1990b). They are characterised by politically biased readings of the archaeological record, which 'demonstrate' the supposed evolutionary distinctiveness and superiority of 'civilised' people of white, Christian, European descent, at the same time as denigrating or denying the cultural achievements of 'other' peoples. They have developed both in Western Europe, and in those parts of the world, such as the 'Orient', 'Africa' and 'Latin America' where archaeology has been practised by colonial groups that have had no historical ties with the peoples whose pasts they have actually been studying. In Britain and France popular atlases of world archaeology published between 1974 and 1988 consistently gave Europe and its Near Eastern roots the greatest coverage, and marginalised other regions of equal archaeological importance on a global scale, such as the Far East, the Americas, sub-Saharan Africa, India, Central Asia and Oceania (Scarre 1990). In former colonial 'Rhodesia', white archaeologists interpreted the large Iron Age settlement of Great Zimbabwe as being built by outsiders, such as the Phoenicians or even the Queen of Sheba, due to their assumption that indigenous black people would have been fundamentally incapable of attaining the level of civilisation suggested by the archaeological remains (Garlake 1982). And in Bolivia, which is politically dominated by the white Portuguese minority, Pre-Colombian archaeological remains have been presented as part of a dead prehistoric past, as part of another ideological strategy to deny the indigenous descendants of the populations who built them a source of historical and religious identity (Mamami Condori 1989).

Re-interpretations of the ruled

In recent years, different groups of oppressed people, including indigenous communities, ethnic minorities and women, have questioned and rejected the politically biased interpretations of the archaeological heritage promoted by those who have dominated them. They have also begun to replace old 'master narratives' with their own histories, in order to enhance their sense of identity and to stake claims to power and economic resources. Some of these new histories reject archaeological approaches in favour of 'living' oral traditions, which carry a sense of local 'authenticity'. But others also draw upon re-interpretations of the archaeological evidence, which retain a sense of scientific authority, for their own vested interests.

Indigenous peoples, especially in post-colonial contexts, have led the way (Layton 1989b; Gathercole & Lowenthal 1990b; Ucko 1990a; Rowlands 1994). Some have reacted strongly against archaeology and its practitioners, who are often perceived to be disrespectful and uncaring outsiders. Others have turned the archaeological 'evidence' of their pre-colonial heritage back upon their former oppressors, particularly in order to demonstrate their own cultural continuity in particular areas, so as to support their claims of territorial ownership, access to sacred and economic resources, and restitution of cultural property. One problem here has been that indigenous archaeologists, often trained in Western academic institutions and funded by Western sponsors, have sometimes absorbed Eurocentric academic perspectives and begun to devalue or criticise their own traditions, and have consequently become isolated within their own communities (Preucel & Hodder 1996b: 611).

Native Americans, in particular, have challenged the authority and relevance of archaeological knowledge, with reference to their own historical evidence, ethnographic reports and oral traditions, of which the latter are rooted in religious belief. As Cecil Antone of the Gila River Indian Tribes said, 'My ancestors, relatives, grandmother so on down the line, they tell you the history of our people and it's passed on ... basically, what I'm trying to say, I guess, is that archaeology don't mean nothing' (Zimmerman 1994: 65). Other Native Americans, such as members of the Hopi Tribe and Navajo Nation, have urged scholars to incorporate oral traditions into their archaeological research, and have highlighted the complementarity of the two forms of evidence, which sometimes converge on certain themes, such as migrations, warfare, residential mobility, land use and ethnicity (Anyon et al. 1997; Echo Hawk 1997). But the majority of archaeologists have rejected oral traditions as a questionable source of historical information, particularly about events dating back more than two or three centuries.

In post-apartheid South Africa, revisionist historians, archaeologists and museologists have also demonstrated the distorted nature of white representations of the introduction of 'civilisation' to the region, at the same time as enhancing the evolutionary status of the indigenous population (Hall 1994; Mazel & Ritchie 1994). They have shown, for example, that far from being a land sparsely peopled by treacherous primitives, South Africa was inhabited for hundreds of thousands of years by well-adapted hunter-gatherers who developed a highly sophisticated cosmology, which they expressed in thousands of paintings on the walls of rock shelters.

In New Zealand, indigenous Maori people have likewise begun to resent the work of archaeologists of European descent, who have built their careers upon the study of Maori culture, history and prehistory, and who have helped to appropriate Maori heritage as the national heritage of New Zealand, giving little in return to local people (Butts 1990; O'Regan 1990). Although they are proud to share their culture with the wider New Zealand society, they also fear that the increasing status of things Maori will lead to the further removal of their heritage by those in power, and to greater white control over their education, resources and decision-making. This situation is not helped by the virtual absence of scholars within the Maori community itself.

Minority groups in 'Western' nations have also found good reason to protest against interpretations of the archaeological heritage that exclude their histories at public archaeological sites and exhibitions. In response to this, some community archaeologists in the USA have begun to develop an 'affirmative' approach to the historical archaeology of minority groups. They follow calls by certain scholars to create a politically active

97

archaeology that challenges the contemporary social order (e.g. Shanks & Tilley 1987a; 1987b; Tiley 1989). A good example of this approach is the African American Project of Archaeology in Annapolis, which set out not only to examine and publicise the previously neglected historical archaeology of black African Americans, but also to transform the social position of its local black constituents (Leone et al. 1995). Since 1988, the project has excavated three sites occupied by free African Americans and one occupied by both enslaved African Americans and their white masters, and has interpreted their material culture by combining standard archaeological methods with the results of interviews with local African Americans. A temporary exhibition was also mounted to raise the public consciousness of the African American archaeological heritage. Mark Leone has optimistically claimed that such an approach is capable of providing: 'a critique of our own society by using its history'; 'a vehicle to give voices to the silenced, power to the disenfranchised, recognition to the ignored, and a historical signature to the anonymous'; and 'a more plural and democratic society' (ibid.: 110). However, some archaeologists have condemned this approach for its use of political ideology.

Feminist archaeologists, seeking social equality and empowerment, have likewise protested at the limited attention paid to the histories of women by white, Western, middle-class, male archaeologists, who have traditionally dominated the archaeological profession. They have also criticised the perpetuation of contemporary ethnocentric and androcentric ideologies in their interpretations of the archaeological heritage, particularly in relation to issues such as the capabilities of men and women, the nature of their power relations and their appropriate roles in society (e.g. Conkey & Spector 1984; Gero 1985; Engelstad 1991; Stig Sørensen 1999). Such androcentrism in archaeological interpretation has some key characteristics. (1) The production of gender-exclusive rather than gender inclusive reconstructions of past human behaviour, with a particular emphasis on male behaviour. (2) An assumption of a relatively rigid sexual division of labour in past societies, which results in the interpretative linking of certain activities with one sex or the other. (3) The placing of different values on the different sexes and their activities, with an overemphasis on the importance of the activities, accomplishments and social lives of those activities presumed to be male, at the expense of the perceptions and experiences of women. As Peter Gathercole and David Lowenthal have pointed out, the 'male-oriented constructions of knowledge have overwhelmingly shaped contemporary archaeological theory, museum presentations and public attitudes' (Gathercole & Lowenthal 1990b: 92). This is evident, for example, in archaeology displays in small museums in Britain where roles for both sexes remain stereotyped, with Roman women commonly represented at the dressing table and Roman men always portrayed as soldiers (Wood 1997).

Alternative interpretations

In addition to rulers and the ruled, there is another large and growing group within contemporary Western society that exhibits a strong interest in interpreting the archaeological heritage according to 'alternative' perspectives. Their interpretative methodologies are commonly characterised by one or more of the following: formal analyses of ancient artefacts and monuments and of ancient myths and legends; generalised cross-cultural comparisons; psychic insights; claims of scientific validity and absolute truth; and claims of establishment persecution (Stiebing 1984; 1995; Feder 1990; 1995; Harrold & Eve 1995). Beyond these basic shared features, however, their beliefs and interpretations are diverse. Here, I shall broadly divide them into five groups: creationists, New Agers, hyper-diffusionists, extra-terrestrialists and Afrocentrists.

Creationism has clashed with archaeological interpretation since the middle of the nineteenth century, when evolutionary geologists and antiquarians first began to question the Biblical account of human origins (Grayson 1983). But it has seen a revival in recent years, particularly in the USA, as a religious-political movement within the New Right (Harrold et al. 1995). Creationists, who tend to be conservative Protestants, basically follow the opening Book of Genesis in the Bible in claiming that the earth is only a few thousand years old, and that humans, along with other living things, were directly created by God in much the same form as they are today. They also oppose evolutionary theories, perceiving them to be a direct threat to their religious faith. The Creation Science Legal Defence Fund has even taken this battle to the law courts, over the question of whether public schools should be legally obliged to assign equal time to the teaching of creationism whenever evolution is taught, as used to be the case in Louisiana (Godfrey & Cole 1995). In 1987, the US Supreme Court narrowly defeated creationist efforts to have the old Louisiana equal-time law reinstated.

In contrast to creationist conservatism, New Agers have incorporated an eclectic mix of counter-cultural phenomena since the 1960s, which together are meant to contribute to a new Age of Aquarius (Shanks 1992: 61). These include a rejection of science, technology, hierarchical power structures and Capitalism, and an interest in matters such as esoteric spirituality, astrology, traditional cultural practices, soft drugs, environmental balance, egalitarianism and the feminine. They trace the origins of these elements in the archaeological record, contrasting the 'consuming materialism, cold science and shattering of the environment' of present times with a vision of the distant past inhabited by 'ancient masters, sensitive to earth forces and aware of cosmic vision, who managed technically brilliant works in stone without disturbing ecological balances'

(Chippindale 1994: 243). Some believe in ancient global catastrophes, and in a great civilisation that once existed on the continent of Atlantis before it was drowned beneath the sea in a giant cataclysm. Others regard the Egyptian pyramids as possessing mysterious powers and hiding cosmic secrets in their measurements. And others are fascinated by ancient religions. Eco-feminists, for example, are interested in goddess-oriented religion, which they trace back to utopian communities in the Copper Age of south-eastern Europe that were eventually destroyed by patriarchal Indo-European invaders (Anthony 1995).

Hyper-diffusionists are much more concerned with issues of cultural and racial origins. They have claimed a single place of origin for all human 'civilisation', ranging from Atlantis to Mu, with reference to similarities between the ancient civilisations of the Old and New Worlds. They have also elaborated diffusionist theories first proposed by racist antiquarians in the late eighteenth and nineteenth centuries, which denied the cultural achievements of indigenous peoples. In the USA, for example, they have attributed the widespread Pre-Colombian monuments that they study, including petroglyphs, mounds and stone ruins, not to the Native Americans upon whose traditional lands these sites are located, but to exotic groups such as the: Egyptians, Mesopotamians, Phoenicians, Libyans, Greeks, Romans and Celts (Downer 1997). Similarly, in Paraguay, the self-styled professor and archaeologist, Jacques de Mahieu, has asserted that the Aché Indians are 'degenerate' descendants of the Vikings, with reference to their unusually light skins, distinctive features and facial hair (Holland 1990).

Extra-terrestrialists, who might be regarded as hyper-diffusionist extremists, go so far as to claim that human beings and their ancient civilisations are the products of visits by ancient spacemen. For example, Erich von Däniken has re-interpreted a complex stylised Maya bas-relief from the site of Palenque,

101

thought by archaeologists to represent a dead king entering the underworld, as a depiction of an astronaut in a rocket ship (Stiebing 1995: 2). However, Native Americans have protested at such interpretations of their cultural heritage, claiming that they are racist in that they denigrate the cultural achievements of their ancestors. The Committee for the Scientific Investigation of Claims of the Paranormal (CSICOP), which was established in Buffalo, New York, in 1976, also provides a strong voice for debunking the claims of extra-terrestrialists, particularly through its journal, *The Sceptical Inquirer*, which has a circulation of 40,000 (Williams 1995: 127).

Afrocentrists share much in common with these hyper-diffusionists, but are also driven by a social struggle for empowerment. They make various claims (Ortiz de Montellano 1995; Howe 1998; Roth 1998). (1) That the ancient Egyptians were black. (2) That the cultural achievements of ancient Egyptian civilisation have been underestimated. (3) That ancient Egyptian civilisation had a much greater influence on Greek and Roman civilisation than has generally been supposed. (4) That ancient Egyptian civilisation originated south of its Pharaonic territory, and maintained and extended those contacts so that all African cultures are related to it. (5) That a black Egyptian civilisation was the impetus for other civilisations such as those of the New World, India and China. (6) That Eurocentric Egyptologists have conspired to hide all this from public knowledge. Like the creationists, Afrocentrists have also made vigorous attempts to introduce their beliefs into school curricula in the USA.

Although they may raise some eyebrows, there is no doubting the popularity of these 'alternative' interpretations of the archaeological heritage. Indeed, their popular appeal is perhaps their most important feature. Their proponents have produced a vast array of publications, many of which have achieved international best-seller status, and their views have received extensive uncritical media coverage. For example, over four million copies of the English version of Erich von Däniken's first book, *Chariots of the Gods*, have been sold (Feder 1995: 44). Moreover, von Däniken still has many followers, especially the 10,000 world-wide members of the Ancient Astronaut Society (Harrold et al. 1995: 153). There are various explanations for the attractiveness of such 'alternative' interpretations (Stiebing 1995). Perhaps most importantly, they provide psychologically satisfying answers for important unknown or unknowable questions that 'Establishment' scientists refuse to answer. At the same time, they appear to be accurate and well documented, at least to the open-minded non-archaeologist. Also, the groups that maintain these beliefs provide a valuable sense of identity for their members. Amateur researchers, writers, publishers and television programmers exploit this demand in their market for 'alternative' histories, attracting large audiences by making their stories as sensational, mysterious and adventurous as possible. The large sums of money that they make on the back of this speak for themselves (Thompson 1999).

In response to this growing popularity of 'alternative' interpretations, busy professional archaeologists have usually chosen to ignore them as 'popular' myths, although a few have painstakingly tried to refute them as 'speculative', 'pseudo-scientific', 'fiction' (e.g. Sabloff 1982; Williamson & Bellamy 1983; Stiebing 1984; Ortiz de Montellano 1995; Roth 1998). They have pointed, in particular, to their ignorance of the stratigraphic, chronological and cultural contexts within which archaeological remains are situated. They have highlighted the racism that is inherent in many of the hyper-diffusionist claims. They have also questioned the Afrocentrists' imposition of contemporary social definitions, such as 'black' and 'African', onto the ancient Egyptian context. However, their efforts have generally met with limited success. Indeed, they have been negative, in that they have tended to confirm their opponents' impression that professional archaeologists are self-serving, authoritarian and elitist.

Interpretive archaeology

How, then, should archaeologists proceed in interpreting the archaeological heritage, particularly in the light of the contemporary proliferation of claims made by different interest groups to the right to re-interpret the material remains of the past? There are no simple solutions. However, I would argue that if archaeologists wish to retain a major stake in the process of interpreting the past on behalf of the public, then they will have to mend and modify their ways. Here are a number of suggestions for the construction of a contemporary 'interpretive archaeology' (Shanks & Hodder 1995).

To begin with, archaeologists must accept that they are fallible. There can never be any final and definitive accounts of the past, given: that 'even when the past was its present it was to a considerable extent incomprehensible'; the fragmentary nature of all archaeological 'evidence'; the necessity of approaching those data with reference to some general theory; and the fact that all archaeological interpretation takes place in present-day cultural, social and political contexts (ibid.). Archaeological interpretation will always involve uncertainty, and it should therefore aspire to being open to change.

Following on from this, archaeologists should welcome the inclusion of a wide range of viewpoints and interpretations, since the greater the range of interpretative options available, the greater the likelihood of correcting bias and eliminating error (Gathercole 1990: 3; Lowenthal 1990: 311). Archaeologists should also acknowledge the criticisms of their interpretations made by people from other cultural traditions, using them to stimulate reconsiderations of the available evidence, rather than dismissing them as unscientific (Layton 1989b: 18). It could be said that 'There are many points of view, many agendas, many voices in archaeology, and room for still more' (Potts 1998: 198-9). Bernard Knapp has adopted this line, for example, in the study of past gender relations, which, he argues, 'must involve both women and men in order to make gender a more dynamic, multifaceted, concept within archaeological interpretation' (Knapp 1998: 247).

Archaeologists must also become more sensitive and responsive to the interests of the local communities amongst which they carry out their research. This responsibility to the public is emphasised in the Archaeological Institute of America's 1990 *Code of Ethics*, which states that 'Archaeologists should make public the results of their research in a timely fashion', and that 'Archaeologists should be sensitive to cultural mores and attitudes, and be aware of the impact research and field work may have on a local population, both during and after work' (Vitelli 1996b: 262-3). But, here, one is still left with the impression that the research interests of the archaeologists remain paramount. This is not the case in the *Ethics Code* of the World Archaeological Congress (WAC), which seeks to ensure that the views of indigenous peoples are taken into account fully by agencies funding or authorising archaeological research (Zimmerman 1994: 68). Some archaeologists have already begun to put this approach into practice in their fieldwork. In the USA, for example, Janet Spector actively enlisted the Wahpeton Dakota people's participation in her archaeological field project at Little Rapids in 1986 (Spector 1991; 1994). As a consequence of experiencing their perspectives, she admits that, 'I became particularly self-conscious about the ways I had learned to write about Indian people, their material culture, and their sites' (Spector 1991: 394-5). In New Zealand, museum archaeologists are showing a growing sensitivity towards Maori people, by recognising the need for consultation with them and for their involvement in all aspects of museum work, both as administrators and as curators (Butts 1990). And in Madagascar, archaeologists were eventually able to win the trust and support of the Betsileo people in the Mitongoa-Andrainjato area in the mid-1980s, by keeping them continuously informed of the results of the field-survey project, and by demonstrating their respect for local oral traditions, knowledge and ritual (Raharijaona 1989).

At the same time, archaeologists must try to engage in open dialogue with the opponents of archaeology. This is, of course, easier said than done, but it should be attempted. As Michael Shanks and Ian Hodder have suggested, 'Talk to people, understand them, persuade if necessary; instead of patronising them by playing the expert' (Shanks & Hodder 1995: 20). Scholars who aggressively denounce 'alternative' interpretations of the archaeological heritage as 'pseudo-science' usually strengthen the other side's hand (Williams 1995: 129; Echo Hawk 1997: 93).

That said, archaeologists should retain an ideal of attempted objectivity in their interpretations of the past. 'Bias is not to be condoned ... simply because it is inherent in any view of the past' (Lowenthal 1990: 311). The surviving physical remains of the past can still be described in terms of 'fact' and 'reality', and as such they impose constraints upon archaeological interpretation. As Alison Wylie says,

> however thoroughly mediated, or 'laden', by theory archaeological evidence may be, it routinely turns out differently than expected; it generates puzzles, poses challenges, forces revisions and canalises theoretical thinking in ways that lend a certain credibility to the insights that sustain objectivist convictions. Consequently, while we cannot treat archaeological data or evidence as a given – a stable foundation – it is by no means infinitely plastic. It does, or can, function as a highly recalcitrant, closely constraining, 'network of resistances'. (Wylie 1992: 25)

5. Interpreting the archaeological heritage

Archaeological interpretations can also aspire to a 'guarded objectivity' by being based upon first-hand experience of archaeological data that are accessible to all; being internally coherent; evaluating material culture with reference to its historical context; and surviving the 'test of time' (Trigger 1995; Thomas 1995: 353-4; Preucel & Hodder 1996a: 528).

Political interests in archaeology do not irrecoverably compromise this commitment to objectivity, in that 'politically engaged science is often much more rigorous, self-critical and responsive to the facts than allegedly neutral science, for which nothing much is at stake' (Wylie 1992: 30). However, archaeologists should aspire to an ideal doing no harm: that is, not prioritising one people's heritage at the expense of another's. In accordance with this principle, archaeologists do, then, have a moral obligation to criticise politically motivated interpretations of the archaeological heritage that use concepts such as 'ethnicity' and 'race' to promote injustice in the present (Layton 1989b: 8; Jones 1996: 75). Whether or not it was justifiable to impose the ban on South African academics attending the first World Archaeological Congress in Southampton in 1986, due to concerns about the freedom of speech and access to academia of black people in apartheid South Africa, is a controversial matter of opinion (Hodder 1986; Ucko 1987). Either way, I no longer favour the suggestion of Michael Shanks and Christopher Tilley that the *only* goal of archaeological research should be a political one (Shanks & Tilley 1987b: 186-208). As Bruce Trigger has noted, 'the history of archaeology reveals that the political uses that have been made of that discipline's "findings" have promoted bigotry, violence and destruction at least as often as they have promoted social justice' (Trigger 1995: 263-4). Above all, this emphasises just how careful archaeologists must be in their interpretations of the archaeological heritage.

6

Experiencing the
archaeological heritage

Archaeologists claim the right not only to study and interpret the archaeological heritage on behalf of the public, but also to be supported by the public to do so. And in general they are. In many parts of the world, professional archaeologists are still provided with substantial amounts of public money to carry out their work. In the UK, for example, archaeologists received over £318 million in the form of state funding in 1999 (Schadla Hall 1999: 152). At the same time, archaeologists generally receive positive media coverage of their activities, which are often portrayed as exciting or sensational. But do archaeologists really deserve all this?

Archaeologists, of course, can put forward a number of general arguments to justify their favourable treatment (e.g. Darvill 1987: 164-7; Adkins & Adkins 1989: 17-19; Trigger 1989: 396-410; Smardz 1990; Fagan 1995b). (1) Archaeologists help to protect and preserve the material remains of the past for the future. (2) Archaeologists rescue information about the past before it is destroyed. (3) Archaeologists respond to people's natural curiosity about past populations and their material remains, providing them with reliable answers about the past at the same time as helping to rid them of any misconceptions. (4) Archaeologists provide interpretations of the origins, diversity and long-term development of human behaviour in the past throughout the world, which help us to understand and respect our own societies in the present and future. (5) Archaeologists contribute to the development of heritage tourism, and hence to local and national economic growth. (6) Archaeology offers educators and their pupils a dynamic resource that helps them to unlock their historical imaginations through an integrated variety of active, interdisciplinary, problem-oriented approaches to learning.

But is this enough? In order to answer this question, it is necessary to examine what the public actually gets in return for their support of the work of archaeologists, particularly in terms of their experiences of the archaeological heritage.

Public experiences of archaeology

People's experiences of archaeology are poorly quantified (Schadla Hall 1999). However, it is clear that people experience archaeology in a wide variety of contexts. These include fieldwork situations, popular publications, heritage sites, museum displays and educational classes. How beneficial such experiences are to members of the public is a matter of debate.

Archaeological fieldwork has traditionally provided local people with the opportunity to experience the work of archaeologists at first hand. In European countries, for example, local people are usually fascinated by on-going archaeological excavations, and often ask whether anything unusual, such as treasure or human bodies, has been found. But such experiences are becoming increasingly limited. The professionalisation of archaeology has led to the marginalisation of these grass-roots supporters and volunteers, who now have few opportunities to participate actively in the archaeological process (Merriman 1991: 103-6; Selkirk 1997). Instead, they are being transformed into passive, voyeuristic, fee-paying, 'visitors': 'You can look, you can even touch, but it's getting harder to join in' (Parker Pearson 1993: 226). This situation is reflected in the

110

UK Institute of Field Archaeologists' 1993 *Code of Conduct*, which makes its priorities clear: 'The archaeologist should be prepared to allow access to sites [but] at suitable times and under controlled conditions, within limitations laid down by the funding agency or by the owners or the tenants of the site, or by considerations of safety or the well-being of the site' (Institute of Field Archaeology 1995: 16). In other parts of the world, local people can be equally interested in the work of archaeologists, although they are often more confused and suspicious about archaeologists wanting to disturb the sacred sites of their ancestors (Nzewunwa 1990: 197). They also commonly want to know how the work of the archaeologists will be of benefit to them, in relation to the maintenance of traditional knowledge and practices; the management and economic exploitation of cultural resources; the provision of employment; the establishment of legal rights to land, water and ancestral remains; and so on (Foanaota 1990: 230; Anyon et al. 1997: 80; Ayres & Mauricio 1999: 306). But, at the same time, they often accuse archaeologists of serving their own academic interests and of giving little in return to local communities. Native Americans, in particular, have vociferously complained that archaeologists' efforts to consult with them during the development of their research designs, and to disseminate the results of their research, have been insensitive and inadequate (e.g. Swidler et al. 1997: 12). As a consequence, many Native Americans continue to ask the same old questions:

> Why do they come and dig up our ancestors? Why do they destroy our ancestors' areas? Why do they destroy our gathering areas? They cannot be trusted! Why are they always writing or telephoning us for information when we do not know who they are? They only want to make money off us! We never get anything in return, not even reports! (Fuller 1997: 146)

Printed publications, films, television and the radio are perhaps the most important contexts in which the public's demand to learn about the work of archaeologists is satisfied. Archaeologists certainly play a part in this process: especially by publishing the results of their research, but also by appearing as experts on television documentaries, such as BBC2's *Chronicle* and *Meet the Ancestors* (Norman 1983; Richards 1999). But such efforts by archaeologists to publicise their work usually reach only restricted audiences. Archaeological publications, for example, which archaeologists rely upon to disseminate the results of their research, are usually designed and written in a particular scholarly style that is inaccessible and boring to non-specialists. As Peter Fowler, a professor of archaeology, admits, 'We write well for ourselves, and sometimes for other specialists and professionals, but we edit out the other 99.99 per cent of humanity' (Fowler 1995: 108). Television documentaries also tend to employ experts to preach to the converted; who, in the UK, are predominantly well-educated, middle-aged, middle-class people (Hills 1993: 223). As a consequence, a large gap exists in the market to popularise archaeology, which is partially filled by a wide variety of journalists, fiction writers and film makers, who inevitably create their own images of the subject and its practitioners. Of these, the most common and durable Western stereotype is that which portrays archaeologists as energetic, adventurous and heroic scientific explorers, who struggle to overcome native obstacles, both natural and human, to reveal long-lost mysterious places, to unlock their secrets, and to remove their hidden treasures. Classic examples include: articles in the *National Geographic Magazine*; Channel 4's *Time Team* television series; Clive Cussler's novel, *Inca Gold* (1994); and Hollywood films such as Steven Spielberg's *Indiana Jones and the Temple of Doom* (1984) (Day 1997). Despite its unsound ideological credentials, which have been criticised by archaeologists as Eurocentric, imperialist and sexist, this old-fashioned image of archaeology has survived extremely well in the popular imagination (Gero & Root 1990; Silberman 1995; Díaz-Andreu & Champion 1996; Solomon 1998). Old films like *One Million Years BC* and *Journey to the Centre of the Earth* also perpetuate a distorted image of prehistory, as a period in which people lived in caves, fought dinosaurs and pulled women around by the hair. Unfortunately, small-scale surveys of public perceptions carried out in England in the mid-1980s indicate that such fictional films, viewed either at the cinema or on television, are the most popular and influential medium through which people learn about archaeology, in contrast to the more reliable but less popular reports provided by 'quality' newspapers, local television programmes and radio programmes (Emmott 1989; Stone 1989). All of this contributes to 'the lack of a broad public understanding of just what archaeology is and does' (Vitelli 1996a: 18).

Archaeological heritage sites provide the public with an opportunity to experience the material remains of past societies at first hand, and for certain groups of people this comprises an important cultural activity. Numbers of visitors to such sites have increased greatly over the last thirty years, particularly as part of a broader enormous growth in heritage tourism. In the UK, for example, there are more than 70 million visits a year to archaeological and historical sites by UK residents; and the prehistoric site of Stonehenge attracted 672,065 visitors in the 1993-94 financial year, each of whom spent an average 'dwell-time' of twenty-five minutes at the site (Ucko 1990b: xix; Bender 1998: 125). Heritage marketers and managers can read increased visitor numbers as increased revenue, but for visitors it is the quality of their experiences that counts. And at English Heritage sites, where the past is packaged according to a highly standardised formula, this quality can be questioned. As Michael Shanks has observed,

There is a very distinctive style to most of these sites. Many are ruins, but consolidated. Loose stones are mortared in position. Walls are cleaned and re-pointed. Paths tended or created. Fine timber walkways constructed. The ground is firm with neatly trimmed lawns. Park benches are provided. This is all justified in terms of health (stopping the further decay of the monument) and safety (of the visiting public). However reasonable such a justification, it creates a distinctive experience of the visit to such an ancient monument. Masonry, grass and sky; such monuments are almost interchangeable, if it were not for their setting. (Shanks 1992: 73)

Furthermore, this package may be attractive to certain types of people, but it is less so to others. For example, a small-scale survey of school-children, aged ten to twelve years old, carried out in the Southampton area of England in the mid-1980s, indicated that although 62% of the children visited historic sites with their parents, children with white and middle-class parents were more likely to be taken to such sites than children with ethnic minority and working-class parents (Emmott 1989: 37). These trends were matched by another survey, of adult daily newspaper readers in the UK, carried out between April 1987 and March 1988, which revealed that readers of the lowest circulating broad-sheet newspaper (the *Independent*, with an estimated readership of 992,000) comprised the highest percentages of visitors to archaeological sites (20%) and historic houses and castles (45%), whereas readers of the highest circulating tabloid newspaper (the *Sun*, with an estimated readership of 11,324,000) comprised the lowest percentages of visitors to archaeological sites (3%) and historic houses and castles (15%) (Ucko 1990b: xx). Local people can also become indifferent to the archaeological heritage that they grow up with, both as a consequence of over-familiarity with it and as a result of its

114

appropriation by politicians and tourists. In Egypt, for example, the Pharaonic pyramids are rarely visited by the residents of Cairo, except during compulsory school excursions, festive occasions and occasional escapes by amorous couples; whereas the Islamic heritage comprises an integral part of contemporary Egyptian life (Hassan 1998).

Archaeological museum displays provide the public with another opportunity to experience the 'real' material culture of past societies, and, like exclusions to heritage sites, visits to them remain an attractive form of cultural activity for large numbers of people. In England, for example, around 4.5 million foreign tourists visited a museum in 1986, amongst which the most popular was the British Museum, which received around 3.8 million visitors in 1985 and around 5.6 million visitors in 1998 (Merriman 1989: 153; Pearce 1990: 34; Windell 1999). Most professional museum curators take their responsibilities towards these visitors seriously, and are becoming increasingly self-critical of their own practices. They are aware, for example, that many members of the public, who are otherwise interested in the past, are deterred from visiting museums by their inherited image as intimidating and elitist 'temples of culture', 'monuments to the dead', 'nationalist shrines' and 'storehouses of obsolete artefacts' (Merriman 1989; Nzewunwa 1990: 194). In the UK, for example, a national survey carried out in 1985 indicated that 'non-visitors' were typically: council house tenants; non-owners of cars; retired, unemployed or part-time workers; and people who attended non-selective schools, which they had left at the minimum age (Merriman 1989: 156). Archaeology curators also know that text-based information is not popular, and that it is not easy to communicate concepts of time-depth and landscape change (Pearce 1990: 195; Cotton 1997: 11). They are equally aware of the power that their displays have to influence people's attitudes towards and interpretations of the past; and that public museum displays of the past continue to exhibit and promote contemporary intellectual, political and social interpretative biases, however unintentional these may be from the perspective of their curators (Blakey 1990; Pearce 1990; Russell 1997).

Educational classes and books on archaeology offer people an additional, indirect, experience of the work of archaeologists and of the archaeological heritage, particularly in relation to the ancient Egyptian, Greek and Roman civilisations of the Mediterranean. But they too have their limitations (MacKenzie & Stone 1990; Ucko 1990b: xv-ii). Over-crowded educational curricula and under-informed teachers often exclude archaeology as a 'luxury' subject of little relevance to today's society. And when they do include archaeology, they often favour certain people's pasts and exclude those of others, in line with contemporary political ideologies that favour certain communities at the expense of others. In the same way, certain periods of history are often promoted above others. In Europe and North America, for example, 'prehistory' is often contemptuously portrayed in school curricula as a period of 'primitive' social relations and limited development, and is usually only considered to be worth studying with reference to the emergence of literate historical 'civilisations'. Furthermore, children's books on archaeology, which are generally not written by archaeologists, frequently misrepresent the archaeological evidence and perpetuate out-of-date racist and sexist interpretations, and yet are often regarded by their readers as sources of factual information (Burtt 1987: 158; Emmott 1989: 37; Planel 1990: 275; Thoden van Velzen & Sofaer Derevenski 1994: 129).

Many people's experiences of the archaeological heritage are not, then, as fulfilling as archaeologists either imagine or would like them to be. In addition to the specific problems raised above, archaeology remains widely regarded as an elitist occupation, carried out by people of leisure and private means, and, in post-colonial contexts, as an activity explicitly related to the former subjection of indigenous peoples (Cleere 1984: 61; Ucko 1990b: xvi). In Lebanon, for example, archaeology, which is mainly perceived as an occupation of the well-to-do and educated, has not been able to generate any significant interest among the population at large, except to encourage the widespread view that the country is full of saleable treasures (Seeden 1990; 1994). In Australia, archaeological studies of Aboriginal history have had little impact on the generally negative public view of Aborigines and their cultural heritage (Barlow 1990: 80). And in England, a national survey carried out on behalf of English Heritage in 1999 revealed that 16% of the public claim to know 'absolutely nothing about Stonehenge, not even what it looks like' (Kennedy 1999).

Blame for this disappointing state of affairs must ultimately be placed with the archaeological profession. Archaeologists are still insufficiently aware of their audiences' cares and concerns (Ucko 1989: xvii). They may also listen too much to their own propaganda (Carman 1995: 97). In the UK, for example, professional archaeologists have generally failed to keep in touch with what the public thinks about the past and about archaeology, and to communicate their findings effectively to this large and predominantly non-academic audience (Stone 1989). Their standard self-justifications of the traditional public support of their activities may still be valid, but they are no longer enough. At a time when government funding for all kinds of cultural activities can no longer be guaranteed, and within the context of the diverse and multicultural societies that we all now live in, archaeologists can no longer afford to take people's support for their activities or experiences of the archaeological heritage for granted (Schadla Hall 1999).

What the public deserves

What kinds of experiences of the archaeological heritage does the public want and deserve, then, in return for their support of the work of archaeologists? Dialogue, access, questions and stories lie at the core of the answers that I favour.

Archaeologists must genuinely consult, communicate and engage in two-way dialogue with people, groups and communities about what they want of their archaeological heritage, rather than patronise them by playing the expert (Shanks 1992; Shanks & Hodder 1995). This means 'taking the popular seriously' (Shanks 1992: 174). As public servants, this is one of the duties and responsibilities of archaeologists (Lynott & Wylie 1995: 23). Of course, different parties will express different interests, but archaeologists must then adhere to the principle of attempting to do no harm. Difficult as it may seem, this strategy can work in practice. In the USA, for example, recent changes to federal and state laws have meant that real discussions are now taking place between American Indians, archaeologists, physical anthropologists and museum people; and that effective collaborative archaeological heritage programmes are now being carried out, particularly amongst the Navajo, Zuni and Hopi in the Southwest (Downer 1997; Zimmerman 1997: 52). Likewise, in Australia, important cultural institutions such as the Australian Institute of Aboriginal Studies and the Australian Museum in Sydney have begun to regard indigenous peoples as 'stakeholders' in their activities (Moser 1995; Specht & MacLulich 1996). As a consequence, real changes can be seen in areas such as: the development of new legislation to protect Aboriginal sites, the practice of site surveys, work on land rights, the employment and training of Aboriginal people in 'responsible positions', the aims of Aboriginal studies, the message of museum exhibitions, the repatriation and reburial of cultural material and the nature of archaeological publications.

Archaeologists must also provide the public with much greater physical and mental access to their work and to the archaeological heritage, in the wide range of contexts where they come into contact with each other (e.g. Binks et al. 1988; Hoffman 1997; Start 1999). Here, I shall focus on the popularisation of archaeology in museums in the UK, where 'access' has become an important priority for increasingly self-critical museum professionals, working within a context of reduced state subsidies and growing competition from the leisure industry. This attitude is clearly reflected in the UK Museums Association's 1998 *Museum Definition*: 'Museums enable people to explore collections for inspiration, learning and enjoyment. They are institutions that collect, safeguard and make accessible artefacts and specimens, which they hold in trust for society' (Museums Association 1998). This perspective can be put into practice in museums with archaeological collections in a number of ways (Pearce 1990). (1) By an emphasis upon seeing the 'real thing'. Objects from the past are principally what museums are about, and it should always be possible to draw out the human interest inherent in them (Longworth 1994: 5-6; Saville 1997: 107). (2) By involving people in a process of self-discovery, linked to their contemporary neighbourhoods, families or cultures. In 1982, for example, the Concord Museum in Massachusetts mounted an exhibition on New England history and culture, which compared seventeenth-century English culture with the Algonquian culture that it encountered, and involved members of the local Chabunagungamaug Nipmuck tribe who provided craft items of traditional design, legends and animal drawings in order to provide the exhibition with a highly successful 'living history' element (Blancke & Peters Slow Turtle 1990). (2) By curating multi-media displays. Visitors respond well to exhibitions which incorporate a range of media,

119

such as differing light levels, contrasting colours, attractive graphics, hierarchical labelling, understandable language, audio-visuals, models, live-guides and so on (Bromwich 1997: 35). (3) By curating interactive exhibitions. Activities like quizzes, computer games and 'hands-on' experiences encourage active participation and help to demystify the work of archaeologists (Owen 1999). An enjoyable example is the award-winning Archaeological Resource Centre (ARC) in York, where families are encouraged to sort through excavated artefacts, look down microscopes, add to computer databases, experiment with ancient technology and ask questions (Moussouri 1998; Jones 1999). (4) By providing access to archives. Seeing 'behind the scenes' not only satisfies people's curiosity and prerogative to know just what is going on in a museum, but also provides curators with a chance to share the interest, and explain the work, involved in managing collections, and so help to justify the public expenditure that such work demands (Stanley Price 1990: 289). (5) By running 'outreach' programmes. Taking small-scale travelling exhibitions to everyday public places such as schools, libraries, building societies and shopping centres is a useful way of making people aware of their local history and of the existence of their museum (Merriman 1989: 168). These can also be targeted at specific groups within the community who may not normally visit museums. Glasgow Museums and Art Galleries, for example, mounted a touring exhibition entitled *In Touch with the Past*, which was intended to introduce various aspects of prehistoric technology to visually impaired people, using about fifty objects from the Museums' reserve collection, ranging from flint-waste flakes, to axe roughouts, to complete polished axes (Batey 1996: 23).

Ultimately, the successful establishment of these kinds of museological programmes depends upon the active involvement of local people, and, above all, on sound 'market' research of visitors and non-visitors. This was the approach that underpinned the excellent refurbishment of the Prehistoric Gallery in the Museum of London in 1994 (Merriman 1996; Cotton & Wood 1996; Cotton 1997). Extensive preliminary research was carried out, which indicated, for example: that people still held numerous misconceptions about the prehistoric period; that the subjects people were most interested in were personal and domestic life, such as living conditions, food, clothing, keeping warm and the role of women and children; and that there was a great demand to be able to handle material. The curators then carefully designed their exhibition with this 'feedback' in mind, with the intention of illuminating prehistory in a 'lively, accessible, honest and … *fun* way' (Cotton 1997: 11). They attempted, for example, to bring the material, historical and social dimensions of prehistoric material culture back to life in people's minds, by displaying objects in specific contexts, and in relation to a large number of two- and three-dimensional reconstructions. They also attempted to explain the processes of environmental change, by incorporating pictures of the changing landscape and sounds of different birdsongs appropriate to each particular environment as a backdrop to successive display cases, and by comparing the familiar contemporary cityscape of London with the very different landscape of prehistoric times. The curators themselves also wished to be explicit about the usually hidden process in which archaeologists move from the material evidence to their interpretations, and about how the latter are historically contingent. They therefore provided a self-critical introductory text-panel, which begins with the question, 'Can you believe what we say?' (Merriman 1996: 64). Alongside this panel is another that critically examines the common preconceptions that people hold about the prehistoric period, accompanied by popular images of the period such as dinosaurs, cave-men from Gary Larson's cartoons and the fur-clad Raquel Welch in *One Million Years BC*. Then, at the end of the gallery, there is a final panel entitled 'Now what does

121

prehistory mean to you?' Visitors' responses to this question are encouraging, in that they indicate that a change in attitude has been encouraged by the new exhibition, with the old stereotypes and misconceptions of the prehistoric period being gradually replaced by more positive concepts. Between 1992 and 1995, there has been, for example, a decrease in the answer 'dinosaurs' (from 28% to 13%), and an increase in the answer 'before written history' (from 5% to 22%) (Cotton 1997: 11).

Providing people with food for thought and encouraging people to think for themselves is, more generally, something that all archaeologists should be doing. Academic archaeologists, for example, can pose unlimited questions about what we are in relation to the object world; archaeology museum curators can help people to think critically about the past and present; and museums' artists in residence can stimulate entirely new ways of seeing the collected material remains of the past (e.g. Shanks 1992: 41-2; Tilley 1989:113-14). But, in doing so, archaeologists should take care not to confuse or irritate their audiences with questions that seem too critical or pretentious (Pearce 1997: 53). This is one of the lessons that Catherine Hills learnt from her experience of working with archaeology on television:

> People arguing with each other should be used sparingly, and the politics of archaeology are not usually gripping to the rest of the world. Things like scientific wizardry, the glamour of golden treasure and the creepiness of skeletons can be used to attract people's attention. But the real point is the story they help to tell about some aspect of how people lived, and what they did, in the past and also in what that tells us about how we are today. (Hills 1993: 224)

Above all, then, it is new stories that people want from archaeologists. This was an important point that Brit Solli realised through questioning local people and visitors about their impressions of her archaeological fieldwork on the island of Veøy in north-west Norway (Solli 1996). In spite of her good intentions and unobtrusive strategies, which stressed dialogue and communication with local storytellers, they all expected her to play the part of the 'expert': to act as the authorised translator and narrator of the material remains of the past, and the teller of tales about how ordinary people used to live on the island. As she noted, 'people of the local community may be willing to participate up to a certain point, but ultimately they would like *you* to tell *them* new stories and not the other way around. The wholly democratic, pluralistic and negotiating archaeology promulgated by Shanks and Tilley ... seems impossible to carry out in practice' (Solli 1996: 225).

Archaeologists must therefore search for the elusive point of balance between playing the expert and being human. Channel 4's *Time Team* television series comes close to succeeding. It is the UK's most popular television archaeology programme, and has been awarded the British Archaeological Award for Best Archaeological Programme twice in a row (Taylor 1998). The cast is headed by a well-known comedy actor, and includes a combination of professional archaeologists, guest experts and local enthusiasts, and the plot is to uncover the secrets of a particular archaeological site in just three days. Although it may perpetuate the myth of the 'archaeologist as hero', and although it treads a fine line between ethical archaeological research and the demands of television drama, it also presents a group of locally-knowledgeable and enthusiastic people with a story to tell, and this is the key to its success. As a consequence, there is 'no need to find a body or a pot of gold' to make the archaeological process interesting to the viewing public (ibid.: 188).

The challenge for archaeologists now is to put some of these ideas into widespread practice themselves, beyond the debating chambers of academia and the glossy brochures of heritage management consultants, with the aim of genuinely enhancing people's real-life experiences of the archaeological heritage. Otherwise, archaeologists will find themselves becoming increasingly marginal to the needs of society in the twenty-first century.

Bibliography

Addyman, P.V., 'Treasure Trove, treasure hunting and the quest for a Portable Antiquities Act', in K. Walker Tubb (ed.), *Antiquities, Trade or Betrayed: Legal, Ethical and Conservation Issues* (Archetype Publications, 1995) 163-72.

Adkins, L. and Adkins, R., *An Introduction to Archaeology* (Quintet Publishing, 1989).

Anderson, D., 'Reburial: is it reasonable?', *Archaeology* 38.5 (1985) 48-51.

Anthony, D.W., 'Nazi and eco-feminist prehistories: ideology and empiricism in Indo-European archaeology', in P.L. Kohl and C. Fawcett (eds), *Nationalism, Politics, and the Practice of Archaeology* (Cambridge University Press, 1995) 82-96.

Anyon, R., Ferguson, T.J., Jackson, L., Lane, L. and Vicenti, P., 'Native American oral tradition and archaeology: issues of structure, relevance, and respect', in N. Swidler, K.E. Dongoske, R. Anyon and A.S. Downer (eds), *Native Americans and Archaeologists: Stepping Stones to Common Ground* (Altamira Press, 1997) 77-87.

Arnold, B., 'The past as propaganda: totalitarian archaeology in Nazi Germany', *Antiquity* 64 (1990) 464-78.

Arnold, B. and Hassmann, H., 'Archaeology in Nazi Germany: the legacy of the Faustian bargain', in P.L. Kohl and C. Fawcett (eds), *Nationalism, Politics, and the Practice of Archaeology* (Cambridge University Press, 1995) 70-81.

Ascherson, N., 'Heritage: a renewable resource?', unpublished paper presented to 'The Idea of Heritage: Past, Present and Future' conference at London Guildhall University (1999).

Ayers, W.S. and Mauricio, R., 'Definition, ownership and conservation of indigenous landscapes at Salapwuk, Pohnpei, Micronesia', in P.J.

Ucko and R. Layton (eds), *The Archaeology and Anthropology of Landscape: Sharing your Landscape* (Routledge, 1999) 298-321.

Bainbridge, S., *Restrictions at Stonehenge: the Reactions of Vistors to Limitations in Access* (Social Survey Division, Office of Population Censuses and Surveys, 1979).

Barber, J. and Welsh, G.M., 'The potential and the reality: the contribution of archaeology to the green debate', in L. Macinnes and C.R. Wickham Jones (eds), *All Natural Things: Archaeology and the Green Debate* (Oxbow, 1992) 41-51.

Barlow, A., 'Still civilizing? Aborigines in Australian education', in P.G. Stone and R. MacKenzie (eds), *The Excluded Past: Archaeology in Education* (Routledge, 1990) 68-87.

Barrett, J.C., *Some Challenges in Contemporary Archaeology* (Oxbow Books, 1995).

Batey, C., 'In touch with the past at Glasgow Museums', in G.T. Denford (ed.), *Museum Archaeology: What's New?* (Society of Museum Archaeologists, 1996) 19-23.

Bator, P.M., *The International Trade in Art* (The University of Chicago Press, 1982).

Begay, R.M., 'The role of archaeology on Indian lands: the Navajo Nation', in N. Swidler, K.E. Dongoske, R. Anyon and A.S. Downer (eds), *Native Americans and Archaeologists: Stepping Stones to Common Ground* (Altamira Press, 1997) 161-6.

Behan, R., 'Solstice ceremony "a farce" ', *Daily Telegraph* 24 June (1998) 5.

Bender, B., *Stonehenge: Making Space* (Berg, 1998).

Binks, G., Dyke, J. and Dagnall, P., *Visitors Welcome: a Manual on the Presentation and Interpretation of Archaeological Excavations* (English Heritage, 1988).

Blakey, M.L., 'American nationality and ethnicity in the depicted past', in P. Gathercole and D. Lowenthal (eds), *The Politics of the Past* (Routledge, 1990) 38-48.

Blancke, S. and Peters Slow Turtle, C.J., 'The teaching of the past of the Native peoples of North America in US schools', in P.G. Stone and R. MacKenzie (eds), *The Excluded Past: Archaeology in Education* (Routledge, 1990) 109-33.

Bland, R., 'The Treasure Act and Portable Antiquities Scheme one year on', *Conservation News* 68 (1999) 25-6.

Bond, G.C. and Gilliam, A., 'Introduction', in G.C. Bond and A. Gilliam (eds), *Social Construction of the Past: Representation as Power* (Routledge, 1994) 1-22.

Born, M., 'Elgin Marbles "staying" ', *Daily Telegraph* 28 July (1999).

Boylan, P.J., 'Illicit trafficking in antiquities and museum ethics', in K. Walker Tubb (ed.), *Antiquities, Trade or Betrayed: Legal, Ethical and Conservation Issues* (Archetype Publications, 1995) 94-104.

Bradley, S.M., 'Do objects have a finite lifetime?', in S. Knell (ed.), *Care of Collections* (Routledge, 1994) 51-9.

Brent, M., 'The rape of Mali', *Archaeology* 47.3 (1994) 26-31, 35.

Brent, M., 'A view inside the illicit trade in African antiquities', in P.R. Schmidt and R.J. McIntosh (eds), *Plundering Africa's Past* (Indiana University Press, 1996) 63-78.

Bromwich, J., 'Displaying archaeology in Britain and France', in G.T. Denford (ed.), *Representing Archaeology in Museums* (Society of Museum Archaeologists, 1997) 29-38.

Brooks, R.L., 'Compliance, preservation, and Native American rights: resource management as a cooperative venture', in N. Swidler, K.E. Dongoske, R. Anyon and A.S. Downer (eds), *Native Americans and Archaeologists: Stepping Stones to Common Ground* (Altamira Press, 1997) 207-16.

Brysac, S.B., 'The Parthenon Marbles custody case: did British restorers mutilate the famous sculptures?', *Archaeology* 52.3 (1999) 74-7.

Burtt, F., ' "Man the Hunter": bias in children's archaeology books', *Archaeological Review from Cambridge* 6.2 (1987) 157-74.

Butler, J., 'The Arts and Antiques Squad', in K. Walker Tubb (ed.), *Antiquities, Trade or Betrayed: Legal, Ethical and Conservation Issues* (Archetype Publications, 1995) 226-8.

Butts, D.J., 'Nga Tukemata: Nga Taonga o Ngati Kahungunu (The awakening: the treasures of Ngati Kahungunu)', in P. Gathercole and D. Lowenthal (eds), *The Politics of the Past* (Routledge, 1990) 107-17.

Byrne, D., 'Western hegemony in archaeological heritage management', *History and Anthropology* 5 (1991) 269-76.

Cannon Brookes, P., 'Antiquities in the market-place: placing a price on documentation', *Antiquity* 68 (1994) 349-50.

Carman, J., 'Interpretation, writing and presenting the past', in I. Hodder, M. Shanks, A. Alexandri, V. Buchli, J. Carman, J. Last and G. Lucas (eds) *Interpreting Archaeology: Finding Meaning in the Past* (Routledge, 1995) 95-9.

Carmichael, D., Hubert, J. and Reeves, B., 'Introduction', in D.L.

127

Carmichael, J. Hubert, B. Reeves and A. Schanche (eds), *Sacred Sites, Sacred Places* (Routledge, 1994) 1-8.

Carver, M., 'On archaeological value', *Antiquity* 70 (1996) 45-56.

Chamberlin, E.R., *Preserving the Past* (J.M. Dent and Sons, 1979).

Champion, T., 'Three nations or one? Britain and the national use of the past', in M. Díaz-Andreu and T. Champion (eds), *Nationalism and Archaeology in Europe* (University College London Press, 1996) 119-45.

Chase, A.F., Chase, D.Z. and Topsey, H.W., 'Archaeology and the ethics of collecting', *Archaeology* 41.1 (1988) 56, 58-60, 87.

Chernykh, E.N., 'Postscript: Russian archaeology after the collapse of the USSR – infrastructural crisis and the resurgence of old and new nationalisms', in P.L. Kohl and C. Fawcett (eds), *Nationalism, Politics, and the Practice of Archaeology* (Cambridge University Press, 1995) 139-48.

Chesterman, J., 'A collector/dealer's view of antiquities', *Antiquity* 65 (1991) 538-9.

Chippindale, C., 'Editorial', *Antiquity* 65 (1991) 3-10.

Chippindale, C., 'Editorial', *Antiquity* 67 (1993) 699-708.

Chippindale, C., *Stonehenge Complete* (Thames and Hudson, 1994).

Chippindale, C. and Gill, D., 'Cycladic figures: art versus archaeology?', in K. Walker Tubb (ed.), *Antiquities, Trade or Betrayed: Legal, Ethical and Conservation Issues* (Archetype Publications, 1995) 131-42.

Chippindale, C., Devereux, P., Fowler, P., Jones, R. and Sebastian, T., *Who Owns Stonehenge?* (B.T. Batsford, 1990).

Ciochon, R. and James, J., 'The glory that was Angkor', *Archaeology* 47.2 (1994) 39-49.

Cleere, H., 'World cultural resource management: problems and perspectives', in H. Cleere (ed.), *Approaches to the Archaeological Heritage: a Comparative Study of World Cultural Resource Management Systems* (Cambridge University Press, 1984) 125-31.

Cleere, H., 'Cultural landscapes as World Heritage', *Conservation and Management of Archaeological Sites* 1.1 (1995) 63-8.

Clément, E., 'The aims of the 1970 UNESCO Convention on the Means of Prohibiting and Preventing the Illicit Import, Export and Transfer of Ownership of Cultural Property and action being taken by UNESCO to assist in its implementation', in K. Walker Tubb (ed.), *Antiquities, Trade or Betrayed: Legal, Ethical and Conservation Issues* (Archetype Publications, 1995) 38-56.

Clover, C., 'Green leaders bridge Newbury divide', *Daily Telegraph* 19 January (1996).

Clover, C., 'Blair insists on cheaper tunnel for Stonehenge', *Daily Telegraph* 23 September (1998) 12.

Clover, C., 'Welcome aboard the Stonehenge experience tour', *Daily Telegraph* 24 April (1999) 8.

Clover, C., 'Stonehenge tunnel row', *Daily Telegraph* 26 June (1999) 11.

Conkey, M.W. and Spector, J., 'Archaeology and the study of gender', *Advances in Archaeological Method and Theory* 7 (1984) 1-38.

Cook, B.F., 'The archaeologist and the art market: policies and practice', *Antiquity* 65 (1991) 533-7.

Cook, B.F., 'The trade in antiquities: a curator's view', in K. Walker Tubb (ed.), *Antiquities, Trade or Betrayed: Legal, Ethical and Conservation Issues* (Archetype Publications, 1995) 181-92.

Corfield, M., 'The reshaping of archaeological metal objects: some ethical considerations', *Antiquity* 62 (1988) 261-5.

Cotton, J., 'Illuminating the twilight zone? The new prehistoric gallery at the Museum of London', in G.T. Denford (ed.), *Representing Archaeology in Museums* (Society of Museum Archaeologists, 1997) 6-12.

Cotton, J. and Wood, B., 'Retrieving prehistories at the Museum of London: a gallery case-study', in P.M. McManus (ed.), *Archaeological Displays and the Public: Museology and Interpretation* (Institute of Archaeology, University College London, 1996) 53-71.

Creamer, H., 'Aboriginal perceptions of the past: the implications for cultural resource management in Australia', in P. Gathercole and D. Lowenthal (eds), *The Politics of the Past* (Routledge, 1990) 130-40.

D'Agostino, B., 'Italy', in H. Cleere (ed.), *Approaches to the Archaeological Heritage: a Comparative Study of World Cultural Resource Management Systems* (Cambridge University Press, 1984) 73-81.

Darvill, T., *Ancient Monuments in the Countryside: an Archaeological Management Review* (Historic Buildings and Monuments Commission for England, 1987).

Darvill, T. and Fulton, A.K., *The Monuments at Risk Survey of England 1995: Summary Report* (Bournemouth University and English Heritage, 1998).

Davies, J.A., 'Preservation and display of archaeological sites in Norfolk: recent work involving Norfolk Museums Service', in G.T. Denford (ed.), *Museums in the Landscape: Bridging the Gap* (Society of Museum Archaeologists, 1998) 46-51.

Day, D.H., *A Treasure Hard to Attain: Images of Archaeology in Popular Film, with a Filmography* (Scarecrow Press, 1997).

Deeben, J., Groenewoudt, B.R., Hallewas, D.P. and Willems, W.J.H., 'Proposals for a practical system of significance evaluation in archaeological heritage management', *European Journal of Archaeology* 2.2 (1999) 177-99.

Dembélé, M. and Van der Waals, J.D., 'Looting the antiquities of Mali', *Antiquity* 65 (1991) 904-5.

Díaz Andreu, M., 'Archaeology and nationalism in Spain', in P.L. Kohl and C. Fawcett (eds), *Nationalism, Politics, and the Practice of Archaeology* (Cambridge University Press, 1995) 39-56.

Díaz Andreu, M. and Champion, T., 'Nationalism and archaeology in Europe: an introduction', in M. Díaz Andreu and T. Champion (eds), *Nationalism and Archaeology in Europe* (University College London Press, 1996) 1-23.

Dietler, M., ' "Our ancestors the Gauls": archaeology, ethnic nationalism, and the manipulation of Celtic identity in modern Europe', *American Anthropologist* 96.3 (1994) 584-605.

Dongoske, K.E. and Anyon, R., 'Federal archaeology: tribes, diatribes, and tribulations', in N. Swidler, K.E. Dongoske, R. Anyon and A.S. Downer (eds), *Native Americans and Archaeologists: Stepping Stones to Common Ground* (Altamira Press, 1997) 188-96.

Downer, A.S., 'Archaeologists–Native American relations', in N. Swidler, K.E. Dongoske, R. Anyon and A.S. Downer (eds), *Native Americans and Archaeologists: Stepping Stones to Common Ground* (Altamira Press, 1997) 23-34.

Echo Hawk, R., 'Forging a new ancient history for Native America', in N. Swidler, K.E. Dongoske, R. Anyon and A.S. Downer (eds), *Native Americans and Archaeologists: Stepping Stones to Common Ground* (Altamira Press, 1997) 88-102.

Ede, J., 'The antiquities trade: towards a more balanced view', in K. Walker Tubb (ed.), *Antiquities, Trade or Betrayed: Legal, Ethical and Conservation Issues* (Archetype Publications, 1995) 211-14.

Eisenberg, J.M., 'The trade in antiquities debate at the Courtauld Institute', *Minerva* 9.1 (1998) 18-19.

Elia, R.J., 'ICOMOS adopts archaeological heritage charter: text and commentary', *Journal of Field Archaeology* 20 (1993) 97-104.

Elia, R.J., 'A seductive and troubling work', *Archaeology* 46.1 (1993) 64-9.

Elia, R.J., 'Conservators and unprovenanced objects: preserving the cultural heritage or servicing the antiquities trade?', in K. Walker Tubb (ed.), *Antiquities, Trade or Betrayed: Legal, Ethical and Conservation Issues* (Archetype Publications, 1995) 244-55.

Ellis, R., 'The antiquities trade: a police perspective', in K. Walker Tubb (ed.), *Antiquities, Trade or Betrayed: Legal, Ethical and Conservation Issues* (Archetype Publications, 1995) 222-5.

Emmott, K., 'A child's perspective on the past: influences of home, media and school', in R. Layton (ed.), *Who Needs the Past? Indigenous Values and Archaeology* (Unwin Hyman, 1989) 21-44.

Engelstad, E., 'Images of power and contradiction: feminist theory and post-processual archaeology', *Antiquity* 65 (1991) 502-14.

English Heritage, *The Monuments Protection Programme: an Introduction* (English Heritage, 1997).

Fagan, B., 'Black day at Slack Farm', *Archaeology* 41.4 (1988) 15-16, 73.

Fagan, B., 'The arrogant archaeologist', *Archaeology* 46.6 (1993) 14-16.

Fagan, B., 'Enlightened stewardship', *Archaeology* 48.3 (1995) 12-13, 16, 77.

Fagan, B., 'Perhaps we may hear voices ....', in Society for American Archaeology, *Save the Past for the Future II: Report of the Working Conference* (Society for American Archaeology, 1995) 25-30.

Fairclough, G., *The Monuments Protection Programme 1986-96 in Retrospect* (English Heritage, 1996).

Fairclough, G., 'Protecting time and space: understanding historic landscape for conservation in England', in P.J. Ucko and R. Layton (eds), *The Archaeology and Anthropology of Landscape: Sharing your Landscape* (Routledge, 1999) 119-34.

Fawcett, C., 'Nationalism and postwar Japanese archaeology', in P.L. Kohl and C. Fawcett (eds), *Nationalism, Politics, and the Practice of Archaeology* (Cambridge University Press, 1995) 232-46.

Feder, K.L., *Frauds, Myths and Mysteries: Science and Pseudoscience in Archaeology* (Mayfield, 1990).

Feder, K.L., 'Cult archaeology and creationism: a coordinated research project', in F.B. Harrold and R.A. Eve (eds) *Cult Archaeology and Creationism: Understanding Pseudoscientific Beliefs about the Past* (expanded edition, University of Iowa Press, 1995) 34-48.

Feilden, B.M. and Jokilehto, J., *Management Guidelines for World Cultural Heritage Sites* (International Centre for the Study of the Preservation and the Restoration of Cultural Property, 1993).

Ferguson, T.J., Watkins, J. and Pullar, G.L., 'Native Americans and archaeologists: commentary and personal perspectives', in N. Swidler, K.E. Dongoske, R. Anyon and A.S. Downer (eds), *Native Americans and Archaeologists: Stepping Stones to Common Ground* (Altamira Press, 1997) 237-52.

Fleet, M., 'A Midsummer nightmare at Stonehenge', *Daily Telegraph* 22 June (1999) 4.

Foanaota, L., 'Archaeology and Museum work in the Soloman Islands', in P. Gathercole and D. Lowenthal (eds), *The Politics of the Past* (Routledge, 1990) 224-32.

Forsman, L.A., 'Straddling the current: a view from the bridge over clear salt water', in N. Swidler, K.E. Dongoske, R. Anyon and A.S. Downer (eds), *Native Americans and Archaeologists: Stepping Stones to Common Ground* (Altamira Press, 1997) 105-11.

Fowler, D.D., 'Cultural Resources Management', *Advances in Archaeological Method and Theory* 5 (1982) 1-50.

Fowler, P.J., 'Archaeology in a matrix', in J. Hunter and I. Ralston (eds), *Archaeological Resource Management in the UK: an Introduction* (Sutton Publishing, 1993) 1-10.

Fowler, P.J., 'Writing on the countryside', in I. Hodder, M. Shanks, A. Alexandri, V. Buchli, J. Carman, J. Last and G. Lucas (eds), *Interpreting Archaeology: Finding Meaning in the Past* (Routledge, 1995) 100-9.

Fuller, R., 'A Me-Wuk perspective on Sierran archaeology', in N. Swidler, K.E. Dongoske, R. Anyon and A.S. Downer (eds), *Native Americans and Archaeologists: Stepping Stones to Common Ground* (Altamira Press, 1997) 143-8.

García Sanjuán, L. and Wheatley, D.W., 'The state of the Arc: differential rates of adoption of GIS for European heritage management', *European Journal of Archaeology* 2.2 (1999) 201-28.

Garlake, P.S., 'Prehistory and ideology in Zimbabwe', *Africa* 52.3 (1982) 1-19.

Gathercole, P., 'Introduction', in P. Gathercole and D. Lowenthal (eds), *The Politics of the Past* (Routledge, 1990) 1-4.

Gathercole, P. and Lowenthal, D., 'The heritage of Eurocentricity: introduction', in P. Gathercole and D. Lowenthal (eds), *The Politics of the Past* (Routledge, 1990) 7-9.

Gathercole, P. and Lowenthal, D., 'Rulers and ruled: introduction', in P. Gathercole and D. Lowenthal (eds), *The Politics of the Past* (Routledge, 1990) 91-3.

Gero, J.M., 'Socio-politics and the woman-at-home ideology', *American Antiquity* 50.2 (1985) 342-50.

Gero, J. and Root, D., 'Public presentations and private concerns: archaeology in the pages of *National Geographic*', in P. Gathercole and D. Lowenthal (eds), *The Politics of the Past* (Routledge, 1990) 19-37.

Gerstenblith, P., 'Unidroit ratified: convention could help protect archaeological sites', *Archaeology* 51.4 (1998) 24.

Ghandhi, S. and James, J., 'The god that won', *International Journal of Cultural Property* 1 (1992) 369-81.

Gill, D.W.J. and Chippindale, C., 'Material and intellectual consequences of esteem for Cycladic figures', *American Journal of Archaeology* 97 (1993) 601-59.

Giridi, A., 'Imperialism and archaeology', *Race* 15 (1974) 431-59.

Godfrey, L. and Cole, J., 'A century after Darwin: scientific creationism and academe', in F.B. Harrold and R.A. Eve (eds) *Cult Archaeology and Creationism: Understanding Pseudoscientific Beliefs about the Past* (Expanded Edition, University of Iowa Press, 1995) 99-123.

Golding, F.N., 'Stonehenge – past and future', in H. Cleere (ed.), *Archaeological Heritage Management in the Modern World* (Unwin Hyman, 1989) 256-64.

Goodman, E. and Suenson Taylor, K., 'Stability, standards and compromises: working with MAP2 in the commercial world', *Museum Archaeologists News* 27 (1998) 3-6.

Grayson, D.K., *The Establishment of Human Antiquity* (Academic Press, 1983).

Guidi, A., 'Nationalism without a nation: the Italian case', in M. Díaz-Andreu and T. Champion (eds), *Nationalism and Archaeology in Europe* (University College London Press, 1996) 108-18.

Hall, M., 'Lifting the veil of popular history: archaeology and politics in urban Cape Town', in G.C. Bond and A. Gilliam (eds), *Social Construction of the Past: Representation as Power* (Routledge, 1994) 167-84.

Hammil, J. and Cruz, R., 'Statement of American Indians Against Desecration before the World Archaeological Congress', in R. Layton (ed.), *Conflict in the Archaeology of Living Traditions* (Unwin Hyman, 1989) 195-200.

Hanley, R., ' "Profiting from the past". Recent heritage developments in the Scottish Highlands', in G.T. Denford (ed.), *Museum Archaeology: What's New?* (Society of Museum Archaeologists, 1996) 55-9.

133

Harrington, S.P.M., 'The looting of Arkansas', *Archaeology* 44.3 (1991) 22-30.

Harrington, S.P.M., 'Bones and bureaucrats: New York's great cemetery imbroglio', *Archaeology* 46.2 (1993) 28-38.

Harrold, F.B. and Eve, R.A., 'Preface to the expanded edition', in F.B. Harrold and R.A. Eve (eds) *Cult Archaeology and Creationism: Understanding Pseudoscientific Beliefs about the Past* (Expanded Edition, University of Iowa Press, 1995) ix-xii.

Harrold, F.B., Eve, R.A. and de Goede, G.C., 'Cult archaeology and creationism in the 1990s and beyond', in F.B. Harrold and R.A. Eve (eds) *Cult Archaeology and Creationism: Understanding Pseudoscientific Beliefs about the Past* (Expanded Edition, University of Iowa Press, 1995) 152-75.

Hassan, F.A., 'Memorabilia: archaeological materiality and national identity in Egypt', in L. Meskell (ed.), *Archaeology Under Fire: Nationalism, Politics and Heritage in the Eastern Mediterranean and Middle East* (Routledge, 1998) 200-16.

Hawass, Z., *The Secrets of the Sphinx: Restoration, Past and Present* (The American University in Cairo Press, 1998).

Hawkes, N., 'Archaeologists put a price on the past', *The Times* 24 February (1998) 12.

Her Majesty's Government, *Ancient Monuments and Archaeological Areas Act 1979* (Her Majesty's Stationary Office, 1983).

Hills, C., 'The dissemination of information', in J. Hunter and I. Ralston (eds), *Archaeological Resource Management in the UK: an Introduction* (Sutton Publishing, 1993) 215-24.

Hingston, A.G., 'U.S. implementation of the UNESCO Cultural Property Convention', in P. Mauch Messenger (ed.), *The Ethics of Collecting Cultural Property: Whose Culture? Whose Property?* (University of New Mexico Press, 1989) 129-47.

Hiscock, J., 'Skeleton site angers sects and science', *Daily Telegraph* 15 April (1998).

Hitchens, C., *The Elgin Marbles: Should they be Returned to Greece?* (Chatto and Windus, 1987).

Hodder, I., 'Politics and ideology in the World Archaeological Congress 1986', *Archaeological Review from Cambridge* 5.1 (1986) 113-19.

Hodder, I., 'Archaeology and the post-modern', *Anthropology Today* 6.5 (1990) 13-15.

Hodder, I., 'Changing configurations: the relationships between theory and practice', in J. Hunter and I. Ralston (eds), *Archaeological*

Resource Management in the UK: an Introduction (Sutton Publishing, 1993) 11-18.

Hodder, I., 'The past as passion and play: Çatalhöyük as a site in conflict in the construction of multiple pasts', in L. Meskell (ed.), *Archaeology Under Fire: Nationalism, Politics and Heritage in the Eastern Mediterranean and Middle East* (Routledge, 1998) 124-39.

Hoffman, B., 'Sevso follies of 1994', *Archaeology* 47.3 (1994) 42-3.

Hoffman, T.L., 'The role of public participation: Arizona's public archaeology program', in J.H. Jameson (ed.), *Presenting Archaeology to the Public: Digging for Truths* (Altamira Press, 1997) 73-83.

Holland, L., 'Whispers from the forest: the excluded past of the Aché Indians of Paraguay', in P.G. Stone and R. MacKenzie (eds), *The Excluded Past: Archaeology in Education* (Routledge, 1990) 134-51.

Howe, S., *Afrocentrism: Mythical Pasts and Imagined Homes* (Verso, 1998).

Howell, C.L., 'Daring to deal with *huaqueros*', in K.D. Vitelli (ed.), *Archaeological Ethics* (Altamira, 1996) 47-53.

Hubert, J., 'A proper place for the dead: a critical review of the "reburial" issue', in R. Layton (ed.), *Conflict in the Archaeology of Living Traditions* (Unwin Hyman, 1989) 131-66.

Inskeep, R.R., 'Making an honest man of Oxford: good news for Mali', *Antiquity* 66 (1992) 114.

Insoll, T., 'Looting the antiquities of Mali: the story continues at Gao', *Antiquity* 67 (1993) 628-32.

Institute of Field Archaeologists, 'Professional standards', in E. McAdam and K. Sisson (eds), *Institute of Field Archaeologists Yearbook and Directory 1996* (Institute of Field Archaeologists, 1995): 14-19.

Jelks, E.B., 'Professionalism and the Society of Professional Archaeologists', in M.J. Lynott and A. Wylie (eds), *Ethics in American Archaeology: Challenges for the 1990s* (Society for American Archaeology, 1995) 14-16.

Jones, A., 'Archaeological reconstruction and education at Jorvik Viking Centre and Archaeological Resource Centre, York, UK', in Stone, P.G. and Planel, G. (eds), *The Constructed Past: Experimental Archaeology, Education and the Public* (Routledge, 1999) 258-68.

Jones, B., *Past Imperfect: the Story of Rescue Archaeology* (Heinemann Educational Books, 1984).

Jones, S., 'Discourses of identity in the interpretation of the past', in P.

Graves Brown, S. Jones and C. Gamble (eds), *Cultural Identity and Archaeology: the Construction of European Communities* (Routledge, 1996) 62-80.

Jones, S. and Graves Brown, P., 'Introduction: archaeology and cultural identity in Europe', in P. Graves Brown, S. Jones and C. Gamble (eds), *Cultural Identity and Archaeology: the Construction of European Communities* (Routledge, 1996) 1-24.

Junker, K., 'Research under dictatorship: the German Archaeological Institute 1929-1945', *Antiquity* 72 (1998) 282-92.

Kaiser, T., 'Archaeology and ideology in southeast Europe', in P.L. Kohl and C. Fawcett (eds), *Nationalism, Politics, and the Practice of Archaeology* (Cambridge University Press, 1995) 99-119.

Kaye, L.M. and Main, C.T., 'The saga of the Lydian Hoard: from Usak to New York and back again', in K. Walker Tubb (ed.), *Antiquities, Trade or Betrayed: Legal, Ethical and Conservation Issues* (Archetype Publications, 1995) 150-61.

Kennedy, M., 'Heritage value is put on "pile of old stones" ', *Guardian* 20 January (1999) 10.

Kimber, A., 'Cultural protection', *Museums Journal* 99.5 (1999) 13.

Knapp, B.A., 'Boys will be boys: masculinist approaches to a gendered archaeology', in D.S. Whitley (ed.), *Reader in Archaeological Theory: Post-Processual and Cognitive Approaches* (Routledge, 1998) 241-9.

Kohl, P.L. and Fawcett, C., 'Archaeology in the service of the state: theoretical considerations', in P.L. Kohl and C. Fawcett (eds), *Nationalism, Politics, and the Practice of Archaeology* (Cambridge University Press, 1995) 3-18.

Kohl, P.L. and Tsetskhladze, G.R., 'Nationalism, politics, and the practice of archaeology in the Caucasus', in P.L. Kohl and C. Fawcett (eds), *Nationalism, Politics, and the Practice of Archaeology* (Cambridge University Press, 1995) 149-74.

Kolen, J. 'Recreating (in) nature, visiting history: second thoughts on landscape reserves and their role in the preservation and experience of the historic environment', *Archaeological Dialogues* 2.2 (1995) 127-59.

Krimgold Fleming, A., 'Securing sites in time of war', in K.D. Vitelli (ed.), *Archaeological Ethics* (Altamira Press, 1996) 128-31.

Lambrick, G., *Archaeology and Agriculture: a Survey of Modern Cultivation Methods and the Problems of Assessing Plough Damage to*

Archaeological Sites (Council for British Archaeology and Oxfordshire Archaeological Unit, 1977).

Lattanzi, G., 'Tales of a *tombarolo*', *Archaeology* 51.3 (1998) 48-9.

Lawson, A.J., 'English archaeological units as contractors', in J. Hunter and I. Ralston (eds), *Archaeological Resource Management in the UK: an Introduction* (Sutton Publishing, 1993) 149-57.

Layton, R., 'Introduction: who needs the past?', in R. Layton (ed.), *Who Needs the Past? Indigenous Values and Archaeology* (Unwin Hyman, 1989) 1-20.

Layton, R., 'Introduction: conflict in the archaeology of living traditions', in R. Layton (ed.), *Conflict in the Archaeology of Living Traditions* (Unwin Hyman, 1989) 1-21.

Layton, R. and Ucko, P.J., 'Introduction: gazing on the landscape and encountering the environment', in P.J. Ucko and R. Layton (eds), *The Archaeology and Anthropology of Landscape: Sharing your Landscape* (Routledge, 1999) 1-20.

Lee, M., 'Despite tribal objections, Interior still plans to date Kennewick Man bones', *Tri-Star Herald* 29 July (1999).

Lee, M., 'Scientists' lawyers renew plea to study ancient bones', *Tri-City Herald* 4 August (1999).

Lee, M., 'Report on Kennewick Man suggests Asian origin', *Tri-City Herald* 15 October (1999).

Leone, M.P., Mullins, P.R., Creveling, M.C., Hurst, L., Jackson Nash, B., Jones, L.D., Jopling Kaiser, H., Logan, G.C. and Warner, M.S., 'Can an African-American historical archaeology be an alternative voice?', in I. Hodder, M. Shanks, A. Alexandri, V. Buchli, J. Carman, J. Last and G. Lucas (eds), *Interpreting Archaeology: Finding Meaning in the Past* (Routledge, 1995) 110-24.

Lipe, W.D., 'Value and meaning in cultural resources', in H. Cleere (ed.), *Approaches to the Archaeological Heritage: a Comparative Study of World Cultural Resource Management Systems* (Cambridge University Press, 1984) 1-11.

Lippert, D., 'In front of the mirror: Native Americans and academic archaeology', in N. Swidler, K.E. Dongoske, R. Anyon and A.S. Downer (eds), *Native Americans and Archaeologists: Stepping Stones to Common Ground* (Altamira Press, 1997) 120-7.

Long, D.L., 'Post-colonial trends in cultural heritage management in Australia and Zimbabwe: towards a non-binary conception of heritage', unpublished paper presented to 'The Idea of Heritage: Past,

Present and Future' conference at London Guildhall University (1999).

Longworth, I., 'Museums and archaeology: coping with chimaera', in D. Gaimster (ed.), *Museum Archaeology in Europe* (Oxbow Books, 1994) 1-8.

Lowenthal, D., 'Conclusion: archaeologists and others', in P. Gathercole and D. Lowenthal (eds), *The Politics of the Past* (Routledge, 1990) 302-14.

Lowenthal, D., ' "Trojan forebears", "peerless relics": the rhetoric of heritage claims', in I. Hodder, M. Shanks, A. Alexandri, V. Buchli, J. Carman, J. Last and G. Lucas (eds), *Interpreting Archaeology: Finding Meaning in the Past* (Routledge, 1995) 125-30.

Lowenthal, D., *The Heritage Crusade and the Spoils of History* (Cambridge University Press, 1998).

Lynott, M.J. and Wylie, A., 'Stewardship: the central principle of archaeological ethics', in M.J. Lynott and A. Wylie (eds), *Ethics in American Archaeology: Challenges for the 1990s* (Society for American Archaeology, 1995) 28-32.

Macinnes, L., 'Ancient monuments in the Scottish countryside: their protection and management', *Scottish Archaeological Review* 7 (1990) 131-8.

Macinnes, L., 'Archaeology as land use', in J. Hunter and I. Ralston (eds), *Archaeological Resource Management in the UK: an Introduction* (Sutton Publishing, 1993) 243-55.

MacKenzie, R. and Stone, P.G., 'Introduction: the concept of the excluded past', in P.G. Stone and R. MacKenzie (eds), *The Excluded Past: Archaeology in Education* (Routledge, 1990) 1-14.

Malone, C. and Stoddart, S., 'Editorial', *Antiquity* 72 (1998) 729-38.

Mamami Condori, C., 'History and prehistory in Bolivia: what about the Indians?', in R. Layton (ed.), *Conflict in the Archaeology of Living Traditions* (Unwin Hyman, 1989) 46-59.

Mazel, A. and Ritchie, G., 'Museums and their messages: the display of the pre- and early colonial past in the museums of South Africa, Botswana and Zimbabwe', in P.G. Stone and B.L. Molyneaux (eds), *The Presented Past: Heritage, Museums and Education* (Routledge, 1994) 225-36.

McCann, W.J., ' "Volk und Germanentum": the presentation of the past in Nazi Germany', in P. Gathercole and D. Lowenthal (eds), *The Politics of the Past* (Routledge, 1990) 74-88.

McGill, G., *Building on the Past: a Guide to the Archaeology and Development Process* (E. and F.N. Spon, 1995).

McGimsey, C.R. and Davis, H.A., 'United States of America', in H. Cleere (ed.), *Approaches to the Archaeological Heritage: a Comparative Study of World Cultural Resource Management Systems* (Cambridge University Press, 1984) 116-24.

McGlade, J., 'Archaeology and the evolution of cultural landscapes: towards an interdisciplinary research agenda', in P.J. Ucko and R. Layton (eds), *The Archaeology and Anthropology of Landscape: Sharing your Landscape* (Routledge, 1999) 458-82.

McGuire, R.H., 'The sanctity of the grave: White concepts and American Indian beliefs', in R. Layton (ed.), *Conflict in the Archaeology of Living Traditions* (Unwin Hyman, 1989) 167-84.

McIntosh, R.J., Keech McIntosh, S. and Togola, T., 'People without history', *Archaeology* 42.1 (1989) 74-81.

Meighan, C.W., 'Burying American archaeology', *Archaeology* 47.6 (1994) 64, 66, 68.

Merriman, J.H., 'Two ways of thinking about cultural property', *American Journal of International Law* 80 (1986) 831-53.

Merriman, J. and Rightmire, G.P., 'Diverse views on the repatriation of human skeletal remains: Larsen Bay and the Smithsonian', *Review of Archaeology* 16.2 (1995) 18-21.

Merriman, N., 'The social basis of museum and heritage visiting', in S.M. Pearce (ed.), *Museum Studies in Material Culture* (Leicester University Press, 1989) 153-71.

Merriman, N., *Beyond the Glass Case: the Past, the Heritage and the Public in Britain* (Leicester University Press, 1991).

Merriman, N., 'Displaying archaeology in the Museum of London', in G.T. Denford (ed.), *Museum Archaeology: What's New?* (Society of Museum Archaeologists, 1996) 60-5.

Merriman, N. and Swain, H., 'Archaeological archives: serving the public interest?', *European Journal of Archaeology* 2.2 (1999) 249-67.

Meyer, K.E., 'The hunt for Priam's Treasure', *Archaeology* 46.6 (1993) 26-32.

Michell, J., *Stonehenge: its history, meaning, festival, unlawful management, police riot '85 and future prospects* (Radical Traditionalist Papers, 1986).

Miles, D., 'Removal of "Seahenge"', *The Times* 11 May (1999) 21.

Miles, D., 'Norfolk timber circle', *The Times* 1 July (1999) 25.

Miller, D., Rowlands, M. and Tilley, C., 'Introduction', in D. Miller, M. Rowlands and C. Tilley (eds), *Domination and Resistance* (Routledge, 1989) 1-26.

Morris, R., 'British archaeology: fifty years on', in M. Heyworth (ed.), *British Archaeology Yearbook 1995-96* (Council for British Archaeology, 1995) 2-6.

Morrison, C., 'United Kingdom export policies in relation to antiquities', in K. Walker Tubb (ed.), *Antiquities, Trade or Betrayed: Legal, Ethical and Conservation Issues* (Archetype Publications, 1995) 205-10.

Moser, S., 'The "Aboriginalization" of Australian archaeology: the contribution of the Australian Institute of Aboriginal Studies to the indigenous transformation of the discipline', in P.J. Ucko (ed.), *Theory in Archaeology: a World Perspective* (Routledge, 1995) 150-77.

Moussouri, T., 'Family agendas and the museum experience', in G.T. Denford (ed.), *Museums for the 21st Century* (Society of Museum Archaeologists, 1998) 20-30.

Museums Association, *Codes of Ethics* (Museums Association, 1997).

Museums Association, *Museum Definition* (Museums Association, 1998).

Naccache, A.F.H., 'Beirut's memorycide: hear no evil, see no evil', in L. Meskell (ed.), *Archaeology Under Fire: Nationalism, Politics and Heritage in the Eastern Mediterranean and Middle East* (Routledge, 1998) 140-58.

Ndoro, W., 'Restoration of dry-stone walls at the Great Zimbabwe archaeological site', *Conservation and Management of Archaeological Sites* 1.2 (1995) 87-96.

Nightingale, J., 'Campaign', *Museums Journal* 99.7 (1999) 5.

Norman, B., 'Archaeology and television', *Archaeological Review from Cambridge* 2.1 (1983) 27-32.

Norman, G., 'Bad laws are made to be broken', in K. Walker Tubb (ed.), *Antiquities, Trade or Betrayed: Legal, Ethical and Conservation Issues* (Archetype Publications, 1995) 143-4.

Norman, G., 'The Trojan War is going on right now', *Daily Telegraph* 27 June (1998).

Nzewunwa, N., 'Cultural education in West Africa: archaeological perspectives', in P. Gathercole and D. Lowenthal (eds), *The Politics of the Past* (Routledge, 1990) 189-202.

O'Keefe, P., 'Conservators and actions for recovery of stolen or unlawfully exported cultural heritage', in K. Walker Tubb (ed.), *Antiquities, Trade or Betrayed: Legal, Ethical and Conservation Issues* (Archetype Publications, 1995) 73-82.

O'Keefe, P., *Trade in Antiquities: Reducing Destruction and Theft* (UNESCO Publishing and Archetype Publications, 1997).

O'Neill, S., 'Sun fails to show for Stonehenge solstice', *Daily Telegraph* 22 June (1998) 8.

O'Neill, S., 'Trust seeks sex ban on chalk giant', *Daily Telegraph* 21 August (1998).

O'Regan, S., 'Maori control of the Maori heritage', in P. Gathercole and D. Lowenthal (eds), *The Politics of the Past* (Routledge, 1990) 95-106.

Ortiz de Montellano, B., 'Multiculturalism, cult archaeology, and pseudoscience', in F.B. Harrold and R.A. Eve (eds) *Cult Archaeology and Creationism: Understanding Pseudoscientific Beliefs about the Past* (expanded edition, University of Iowa Press, 1995) 134-51.

Owen, J., 'Interaction or tokenism? The role of "hands-on activities" in museum archaeology displays', in Merriman, N. (ed.), *Making Early Histories in Museums* (Leicester University Press, 1999) 173-89.

Palmer, N., 'Recovering stolen art', in K. Walker Tubb (ed.), *Antiquities, Trade or Betrayed: Legal, Ethical and Conservation Issues* (Archetype Publications, 1995) 1-37.

Papageorge Kouroupas, M., 'United States efforts to protect cultural property: implementation of the 1970 UNESCO Convention', in K. Walker Tubb (ed.), *Antiquities, Trade or Betrayed: Legal, Ethical and Conservation Issues* (Archetype Publications, 1995) 83-93.

Parker Pearson, M., 'Visitors welcome', in J. Hunter and I. Ralston (eds), *Archaeological Resource Management in the UK: an Introduction* (Sutton Publishing, 1993) 225-31.

Paterson, R.K., 'The "Curse of the London Nataraja" ', *International Journal of Cultural Property* 5 (1996) 330-8.

Pearce, S.M., *Archaeological Curatorship* (Leicester University Press, 1990).

Pearce, S.M., 'Archaeology as collection', in G.T. Denford (ed.), *Representing Archaeology in Museums* (Society of Museum Archaeologists, 1997) 47-54.

Pinkerton, L.F., 'The Native American Graves Protection and Repatriation Act: an introduction', *International Journal of Cultural Property* 1 (1992) 297-305.

Pitts, M., 'Manifesto for a green archaeology', in L. Macinnes and C.R.

Wickham Jones (eds), *All Natural Things: Archaeology and the Green Debate* (Oxbow, 1992) 203-13.

Planel, P., 'New Archaeology, New History – when will they meet? Archaeology in English secondary schools', in P.G. Stone and R. MacKenzie (eds), *The Excluded Past: Archaeology in Education* (Routledge, 1990) 271-81.

Potts, D.T., 'The Gulf Arab states and their archaeology', in L. Meskell (ed.), *Archaeology Under Fire: Nationalism, Politics and Heritage in the Eastern Mediterranean and Middle East* (Routledge, 1998) 189-99.

Preucel, R.W. and Hodder, I., 'Representations and antirepresentations', in R.W. Preucel and I. Hodder (eds), *Contemporary Archaeology in Theory: a Reader* (Blackwell Publishers, 1996) 519-30.

Preucel, R.W. and Hodder, I., 'Constructing identities', in R.W. Preucel and I. Hodder (eds), *Contemporary Archaeology in Theory: a Reader* (Blackwell Publishers, 1996) 601-14.

Price, N., 'Tourism and the Bighorn Medicine Wheel: how multiple use does not work for sacred land sites', in D.L. Carmichael, J. Hubert, B. Reeves and A. Schanche (eds), *Sacred Sites, Sacred Places* (Routledge, 1994) 259-64.

Prott, L.V., 'National and international laws on the protection of the cultural heritage', in K. Walker Tubb (ed.), *Antiquities, Trade or Betrayed: Legal, Ethical and Conservation Issues* (Archetype Publications, 1995) 57-72.

Prott, L.V. and O'Keefe, P.J., ' "Cultural heritage" or "cultural property"?', *International Journal of Cultural Property* 1 (1992) 307-19.

Purves, L., 'A transient beauty', *The Times* 29 June (1999) 20.

Pwiti, G., 'Let the ancestors rest in peace? New challenges for cultural heritage management in Zimbabwe', *Conservation and Management of Archaeological Sites* 1.2 (1995) 151-60.

Raharijaona, V., 'Archaeology and oral traditions in the Mitongoa-Andrainjato area (Betsileo region of Madagascar)', in R. Layton (ed.), *Who Needs the Past? Indigenous Values and Archaeology* (Unwin Hyman, 1989) 189-94.

Rapu, S., 'Fifty years of conservation experience on Easter Island (Rapa Nui), Chile', in P. Gathercole and D. Lowenthal (eds), *The Politics of the Past* (Routledge, 1990)

Ravesloot, J.C., 'Changing Native American perceptions of archaeology and archaeologists', in N. Swidler, K.E. Dongoske, R. Anyon and

A.S. Downer (eds), *Native Americans and Archaeologists: Stepping Stones to Common Ground* (Altamira Press, 1997) 172-7.

Reichstein, J., 'Federal Republic of Germany', in H. Cleere (ed.), *Approaches to the Archaeological Heritage: a Comparative Study of World Cultural Resource Management Systems* (Cambridge University Press, 1984) 37-47.

Renfrew, C., 'Introduction', in K. Walker Tubb (ed.), *Antiquities, Trade or Betrayed: Legal, Ethical and Conservation Issues* (Archetype Publications, 1995) xvii-xxi.

Renfrew, C., *Loot, Legitimacy and Ownership: the Ethical Crisis in Archaeology* (Stichting Nederlands Museum Voor Anthropologie en Praehistorie, 1999).

Reynolds, N., 'Elgin Marbles could go home', *Daily Telegraph* 3 April (1996) 4.

Reynolds, N., 'Curator comes clean over Elgin Marbles', *Daily Telegraph* 1 December (1999).

Richards, J., *Meet the Ancestors: Unearthing the Evidence that Brings Us Face to Face with the Past* (BBC Worldwide, 1999).

Ritchie, D., 'Principles and practice of site protection laws in Australia', in D.L. Carmichael, J. Hubert, B. Reeves and A. Schanche (eds), *Sacred Sites, Sacred Places* (Routledge, 1994) 227-44.

Romer, J. and Romer, E., *The Rape of Tutankhamun* (Michael O'Mara Books, 1993).

Rose, M., 'Hoard returned', *Archaeology* 52.3 (1999) 28.

Rose, M. and Acar, Ö., 'Turkey's war on the illicit antiquities trade', *Archaeology* 48.2 (1995) 45-50, 52-3, 55-6.

Roth, A.M., 'Ancient Egypt in America: claiming the riches', in L. Meskell (ed.), *Archaeology Under Fire: Nationalism, Politics and Heritage in the Eastern Mediterranean and Middle East* (Routledge, 1998) 217-29.

Rowlands, M., 'The archaeology of colonialism and constituting the African peasantry', in D. Miller, M. Rowlands and C. Tilley (eds), *Domination and Resistance* (Routledge, 1989) 261-83.

Rowlands, M., 'The politics of identity in archaeology', in G.C. Bond and A. Gilliam (eds), *Social Construction of the Past: Representation as Power* (Routledge, 1994) 129-43.

Russell, L., 'Focusing on the past: visual and textual images of Aboriginal Australia in museums', in B.L. Molyneaux (ed.), *The Cultural Life of Images: Visual Representation in Archaeology* (Routledge, 1997) 230-48.

Sabloff, J., 'Introduction', in J. Sabloff (ed.), *Archaeology: Myth and Reality* (W.H. Freeman and Company, 1982) 1-26.

Sanogo, K., 'The looting of cultural material in Mali', *Culture Without Context* 4 (1999) 21-5.

Saville, A., 'Thinking *things* over after the 1995 SMA conference', in G.T. Denford (ed.), *Representing Archaeology in Museums* (Society of Museum Archaeologists, 1997) 101-10.

Scarre, C., 'The Western world view in archaeological atlases', in P. Gathercole and D. Lowenthal (eds), *The Politics of the Past* (Routledge, 1990) 11-18.

Schadla Hall, T., 'Antiquities legislation: a proper basis?', in G.T. Denford (ed.), *Museum Archaeology: What's New?* (Society of Museum Archaeologists, 1996) 12-16.

Schadla Hall, T., 'Editorial: public archaeology', *European Journal of Archaeology* 2.2 (1999) 147-58.

Schmidt, H., 'Reconstruction of ancient buildings', in M. De La Torre (ed.), *The Conservation of Archaeological Sites in the Mediterranean Region* (The Getty Conservation Institute, 1997) 41-50.

Schmidt, P.R. and McIntosh, R.J., 'The African past endangered', in P.R. Schmidt and R.J. McIntosh (eds), *Plundering Africa's Past* (Indiana University Press, 1996) 1-17.

Scott, S., 'St. Lawrence: archaeology of a Bering Sea island', *Archaeology* 37.1 (1984) 46-52.

Seeden, H., 'Search for the missing link: archaeology and the public in Lebanon', in P. Gathercole and D. Lowenthal (eds), *The Politics of the Past* (Routledge, 1990) 141-59.

Seeden, H., 'Archaeology and the public in Lebanon: developments since 1986', in P.G. Stone and B.L. Molyneaux (eds), *The Presented Past: Heritage, Museums and Education* (Routledge, 1994) 95-108.

Selkirk, A., *Who Owns the Past? A Grass Roots Critique of Heritage Policy* (Adam Smith Institute, 1997).

Shanks, M., *Experiencing the Past: on the Character of Archaeology* (Routledge, 1992).

Shanks, M. and Hodder, I., 'Processual, postprocessual and interpretive archaeologies', in I. Hodder, M. Shanks, A. Alexandri, V. Buchli, J. Carman, J. Last and G. Lucas (eds), *Interpreting Archaeology: Finding Meaning in the Past* (Routledge, 1995) 3-29.

Shanks, M. and Tilley, C., *Re-Constructing Archaeology: Theory and Practice* (Cambridge University Press, 1987).

144

Shanks, M. and Tilley, C., *Social Theory and Archaeology* (Polity Press, 1987).

Sheldon, H., 'The lure of loot: an example or two', in K. Walker Tubb (ed.), *Antiquities, Trade or Betrayed: Legal, Ethical and Conservation Issues* (Archetype Publications, 1995) 176-80.

Shennan, S.J., 'Introduction: archaeological approaches to cultural identity', in S.J. Shennan (ed.), *Archaeological Approaches to Cultural Identity* (Unwin Hyman, 1989) 1-32.

Sheridan, A., 'Portable antiquities legislation in Scotland: what is it, and how well does it work?', in K. Walker Tubb (ed.), *Antiquities, Trade or Betrayed: Legal, Ethical and Conservation Issues* (Archetype Publications, 1995) 193-204.

Shnirelman, V.A., 'The faces of nationalist archaeology in Russia', in M. Díaz-Andreu and T. Champion (eds), *Nationalism and Archaeology in Europe* (University College London Press, 1996) 218-42.

Shore, C., 'Imagining the new Europe: identity and heritage in European Community discourse', in P. Graves Brown, S. Jones and C. Gamble (eds), *Cultural Identity and Archaeology: the Construction of European Communities* (Routledge, 1996) 96-115.

Sidibé, S., 'The fight against the plundering of Malian cultural heritage and illicit exploration', in P.R. Schmidt and R.J. McIntosh (eds), *Plundering Africa's Past* (Indiana University Press, 1996) 79-86.

Silberman, N.A., 'Promised lands and chosen peoples: the politics and poetics of archaeological narrative', in P.L. Kohl and C. Fawcett (eds), *Nationalism, Politics, and the Practice of Archaeology* (Cambridge University Press, 1995) 249-62.

Simpson, M.G., *Making Representations: Museums in the Post-Colonial Era* (Routledge, 1996).

Slayman, A.L., 'Khmer site looted', *Archaeology* 52.3 (1999) 31.

Slayman, A.L., 'Mass reburial', *Archaeology* 52.4 (1999) 17.

Smardz, K., 'Archaeology in the Toronto school system: the Archaeological Resource Centre', in P.G. Stone and R. MacKenzie (eds), *The Excluded Past: Archaeology in Education* (Routledge, 1990) 293-307.

Smith, H., 'Lost marbles: tourists targeted in Greek campaign to retrieve sculptures', *Guardian* Saturday August 14 (1999) 9.

Solli, B., 'Narratives of Veøy: on the poetics and scientifics of archaeology', in P. Graves Brown, S. Jones and C. Gamble (eds), *Cultural*

Identity and Archaeology: the Construction of European Communities (Routledge, 1996) 209-27.

Solomon, J., 'Decades of make believe: Hollywood portraits of the archaeologist as vulnerable romantic or adventure hero', *Archaeology* 51.5 (1998) 92-5.

Specht, J. and MacLulich, C., 'Changes and challenges: the Australian Museum and indigenous communities', in P.M. McManus (ed.), *Archaeological Displays and the Public: Museology and Interpretation* (Institute of Archaeology, University College London, 1996) 27-49.

Spector, J.D., 'What this awl means: toward a feminist archaeology', in J.M. Gero and M.W. Conkey (eds), *Engendering Archaeology: Women and Prehistory* (Basil Blackwell, 1991) 388-406.

Spector, J.D., 'Collaboration at *Inyan Ceyaka Atonwan* (Village at the Rapids)', *Society for American Archaeology Bulletin* 12.3 (1994) 8-10.

Spencer, P., 'Not poachers, rather fellow gamekeepers', *Museums Journal* 98.4 (1998) 20-1.

Spriggs, M., 'God's police and damned whores: images of archaeology in Hawaii', in P. Gathercole and D. Lowenthal (eds), *The Politics of the Past* (Routledge, 1990) 118-29.

Staley, D.P., 'St. Lawrence Island's subsistence diggers: a new perspective on human effects on archaeological sites', *Journal of Field Archaeology* 20 (1993) 347-55.

Stanley Price, N.P., 'Conservation and information in the display of prehistoric sites', in P. Gathercole and D. Lowenthal (eds), *The Politics of the Past* (Routledge, 1990) 284-90.

Stanley Price, N. and Sullivan, S., 'Conservation of archaeological sites in the Mediterranean region', *Conservation and Management of Archaeological Sites* 1.2 (1995) 127-31.

Start, D., 'Community archaeology: bringing it back to local communities', in G. Chitty and D. Baker (eds), *Managing Historic Sites and Buildings: Reconciling Presentation and Preservation* (Routledge, 1999) 49-59.

Staunton, M., *Stonehenge: a Report into the Civil Liberties Implications of the Events Relating to the Convoys of Summer 1985 and 1986* (National Council for Civil Liberties, 1986).

St Clair, W., *Lord Elgin and the Marbles* (3rd edition, Oxford University Press, 1998).

Stiebing, W.H., *Ancient Astronauts, Cosmic Collisions, and Other Popular Theories About Man's Past* (Prometheus Books, 1984).

Stiebing, W.H., 'The nature and dangers of cult archaeology', in F.B. Harrold and R.A. Eve (eds) *Cult Archaeology and Creationism: Understanding Pseudoscientific Beliefs about the Past* (expanded edition, University of Iowa Press, 1995) 1-10.

Stig Sørensen, M.L., 'Archaeology, gender and the museum', in Merriman, N. (ed.), *Making Early Histories in Museums* (Leicester University Press, 1999) 136-50.

Stone, P.G., 'Interpretations and uses of the past in modern Britain and Europe. Why are people interested in the past? Do experts know or care? A plea for further study', in R. Layton (ed.), *Who Needs the Past? Indigenous Values and Archaeology* (Unwin Hyman, 1989) 195-206.

Stone, P.G., 'The Stonehenge we deserve?', *Minerva* 10.3 (1999) 22-5.

Swain, H., 'Archaeological archive transfer in England, theory and practice', in G.T. Denford (ed.), *Representing Archaeology in Museums* (Society of Museum Archaeologists, 1997) 122-44.

Swain, H., 'The national survey of archaeological archives: an interim statement', *Museum Archaeologists News* 25 (1997) 1-3.

Swidler, N. and Cohen, J., 'Issues in intertribal consultation', in N. Swidler, K.E. Dongoske, R. Anyon and A.S. Downer (eds), *Native Americans and Archaeologists: Stepping Stones to Common Ground* (Altamira Press, 1997) 197-206.

Swidler, N., Dongoske, K.E., Anyon, R. and Downer, A.S., 'Preface and acknowledgements', in N. Swidler, K.E. Dongoske, R. Anyon and A.S. Downer (eds), *Native Americans and Archaeologists: Stepping Stones to Common Ground* (Altamira Press, 1997) 11-15.

Taylor, T., *Behind the Scenes at Time Team* (Channel 4 Books, 1998).

Thoden van Velzen, D., 'The world of Tuscan tomb robbers: living with the local community and the ancestors', *International Journal of Cultural Property* 5 (1996) 111-26.

Thoden van Velzen, D. and Sofaer Derevenski, J., 'Book reviews for and by children', *Archaeological Review from Cambridge* 13.2 (1994) 129-43.

Thomas, J., 'Where are we now? Archaeological theory in the 1990s', in P.J. Ucko (ed.), *Theory in Archaeology: a World Perspective* (Routledge, 1995) 343-62.

Thomas, R., 'Welcome mat out for London's archaeology', *Museums Journal* 98.9 (1998) 9.

Thompson, D., 'Minoans built Stonehenge, Atlantis is based in Antarctica, Jesus was buried in France: welcome to the bestselling world of bogus archaeology', *Daily Telegraph* 7 August (1999) 1.

Tilley, C., 'Archaeology as socio-political action in the present', in V. Pinsky and A. Wylie (eds), *Critical Traditions in Contemporary Archaeology: Essays in the Philosophy, History and Socio-politics of Archaeology* (Cambridge University Press, 1989) 104-16.

Trigger, B.G., 'Alternative archaeologies: nationalist, colonialist, imperialist', *Man* 19 (1984) 355-70.

Trigger, B.G., *A History of Archaeological Thought* (Cambridge University Press, 1989).

Trigger, B.G., 'Romanticism, nationalism, and archaeology', in P.L. Kohl and C. Fawcett (eds), *Nationalism, Politics, and the Practice of Archaeology* (Cambridge University Press, 1995) 263-79.

Trolle Larsen, M., 'Orientalism and Near Eastern archaeology', in D. Miller, M. Rowlands and C. Tilley (eds), *Domination and Resistance* (Routledge, 1989) 229-39.

Tsosie, R., 'Indigenous rights and archaeology', in N. Swidler, K.E. Dongoske, R. Anyon and A.S. Downer (eds), *Native Americans and Archaeologists: Stepping Stones to Common Ground* (Altamira Press, 1997) 64-76.

Ucko, P.J., *Academic Freedom and Apartheid: the Story of the World Archaeological Congress* (Duckworth, 1987).

Ucko, P.J., 'Foreword', in R. Layton (ed.), *Conflict in the Archaeology of Living Traditions* (Unwin Hyman, 1989) ix-xvii.

Ucko, P.J., 'Foreword', in P. Gathercole and D. Lowenthal (eds), *The Politics of the Past* (Routledge, 1990) ix-xxi.

Ucko, P.J., 'Foreword', in P.G. Stone and R. MacKenzie (eds), *The Excluded Past: Archaeology in Education* (Routledge, 1990) ix-xxiv.

Ucko, P.J., 'Foreword', in D.L. Carmichael, J. Hubert, B. Reeves and A. Schanche (eds), *Sacred Sites, Sacred Places* (Routledge, 1994) xiii-xxiii.

UNESCO, *The Convention* (UNESCO, 1997).

Vitelli, K.D., 'Introductio', in K.D. Vitelli (ed.), *Archaeological Ethics* (Altamira Press, 1996) 17-28.

Vitelli, K.D., 'Statements on archaeological ethics from professional organizations', in K.D. Vitelli (ed.), *Archaeological Ethics* (Altamira Press, 1996) 253-65.

Wade Martins, P., 'Monument conservation through land purchase', *Conservation Bulletin* 29 (1996) 8-11.

Wainwright, G., 'Stonehenge saved?', *Antiquity* 70 (1996) 9-12.

Wainwright, M., 'Heritage all at sea: Druids take on archaeologists', *Guardian* 16 June (1999) 6.

Walker Tubb, K., 'The antiquities trade: an archaeological conservator's perspective', in K. Walker Tubb (ed.), *Antiquities, Trade or Betrayed: Legal, Ethical and Conservation Issues* (Archetype Publications, 1995) 256-63.

Walster, A., 'The rock art project – part two: "stoned again!" ', *Conservation News* 61 (1996) 35-8.

Warren, K.J., 'A philosophical perspective on the ethics and resolution of cultural property issues', in P. Mauch Messenger (ed.), *The Ethics of Collecting Cultural Property: Whose Culture? Whose Property?* (University of New Mexico Press, 1989) 1-25.

Watson, P., *Sotheby's: Inside Story* (Bloomsbury, 1997).

White Deer, G., 'Return of the sacred: spirituality and the scientific imperative', in N. Swidler, K.E. Dongoske, R. Anyon and A.S. Downer (eds), *Native Americans and Archaeologists: Stepping Stones to Common Ground* (Altamira Press, 1997) 37-43.

Whittell, G., 'Bones put Indians on warpath', *The Times* 4 October (1997) 19.

Willems, W.J.H., 'Archaeology and heritage management in Europe: trends and developments', *European Journal of Archaeology* 1.3 (1998) 293-311.

Williams, S., 'Fantastic archaeology: what should we do about it?', in F.B. Harrold and R.A. Eve (eds) *Cult Archaeology and Creationism: Understanding Pseudoscientific Beliefs about the Past* (expanded edition, University of Iowa Press, 1995) 124-33.

Williamson, T. and Bellamy, L., *Ley Lines in Question* (World's Work, 1983).

Wilson, D.M., *The British Museum: Purpose and Politics* (The Trustees of the British Museum, 1989).

Windell, J., 'Heritage visits remain constant', *Museums Journal* 99.6 (1999) 15.

Wiwjorra, I., 'German archaeology and its relation to nationalism and racism', in M. Díaz-Andreu and T. Champion (eds), *Nationalism and Archaeology in Europe* (University College London Press, 1996) 164-88.

Wood, B., 'Does size matter? Effective presentation of archaeology in small museums', in G.T. Denford (ed.), *Representing Archaeology in Museums* (Society of Museum Archaeologists, 1997) 59-64.

Woolf, M., 'Greeks to inspect the Elgin Marbles', *Daily Telegraph* 27 October (1999) 5.

Wylie, A., 'The interplay of evidential constraints and political interests: recent archaeological research on gender', *American Antiquity* 57 (1992) 15-35.

Young, C. 'Hadrian's Wall', in G. Chitty and D. Baker (eds), *Managing Historic Sites and Buildings: Reconciling Presentation and Preservation* (Routledge, 1999) 35-48.

Zimmerman, L.J., 'Made radical by my own: an archaeologist learns to accept reburial', in R. Layton (ed.), *Conflict in the Archaeology of Living Traditions* (Unwin Hyman, 1989) 60-7.

Zimmerman, L.J., 'Human bones as symbols of power: aboriginal American belief systems toward bones and "grave-robbing" archaeologists', in R. Layton (ed.), *Conflict in the Archaeology of Living Traditions* (Unwin Hyman, 1989) 211-16.

Zimmerman, L.J., 'Sharing control of the past', *Archaeology* 47.6 (1994) 65, 67-8.

Zimmerman, L.J., 'Remythologizing the relationship between Indians and archaeologists', in N. Swidler, K.E. Dongoske, R. Anyon and A.S. Downer (eds), *Native Americans and Archaeologists: Stepping Stones to Common Ground* (Altamira Press, 1997) 44-56.

Index

access: 118-19; to academia, 107;
to archaeological sites, 14,
81, 86, 111; to economic
resources, 96; to museum
collections, 24, 70-1, 120-1; to
sacred sites, 60, 77, 81-4, 96
acquisition: by collectors, 49; by
museums, 49, 71; by nations,
32, 43; of sites, 67
Acropolis, 31, 34-6, 64
African American Project of
Archaeology, 98
African Burial Ground
Memorial, 30
Afrocentrists, 99, 102-3
American Committee for
Preservation of
Archaeological Collections,
24
American Indian tribes: Aché,
101; Alonquian, 119; Central
Sierra Me-Wuk, 87;
Chabunagungamaug
Nipmuck, 119; Gila River, 96;
Hopi, 96, 118; Navajo Nation,
80, 96, 118; Suquamish, 21;
Umatilla, 28; Wahpeton
Dakota, 105; Yupik, 59; Zuni,
118

American Indians Against
Desecration, 23
ancestors, 9, 21-5, 28-9, 32, 59,
68, 96, 102, 111
Ancient Astronaut Society, 103
anthropologists: social, 25, 82;
physical, 19-20, 24, 28, 118
antiquarians, 100-1
antiquities: 9, 12, 19; dealers,
40-1, 46-9, 53-4; trade, 39-55
Antone, Cecil, 96
Archaeological Conservancy,
66-7
Archaeological Institute of
America, 50, 105
Archaeological Resource Centre,
120
archaeological: collections, 15;
consultancies, 29, 124;
excavation archives, 70-1, 76,
84; excavations, 22, 26-31,
48-9, 55-6, 69, 74-6, 80, 92,
98; fieldwork, 25, 55, 61, 63,
65, 72-3, 75-6, 86, 105-6, 110,
123; parks, 72, 75-6, 82;
record, 15, 94, 100; recording,
15-17, 55-6, 62-3, 75; reports,
15, 75, 80, 111; research, 10,
17, 24-5, 27-8, 58, 75, 89, 94,

151